Successful
Instructional
Diagrams

Successful Instructional Diagrams

RIC LOWE

KOGAN PAGE

London • Philadelphia
Published in association with the AETT

First published in 1993

Apart from any fair dealing for the purposes of research or private study, or criticism or review, as permitted under the Copyright, Designs and Patents Act, 1988, this publication may only be reproduced, stored or transmitted, in any form or by any means, with the prior permission in writing of the publishers, or in the case of reprographic reproduction in accordance with the terms of licences issued by the Copyright Licensing Agency. Enquiries concerning reproduction outside those terms should be sent to the publishers at the undermentioned address:

Kogan Page Limited
120 Pentonville Road
London N1 9JN

© Ric Lowe, 1993

Figures 1.1, 1.2 and 1.3 are used with the kind permission of
The Australian Journal of Reading.

British Library Cataloguing in Publication Data

A CIP record for this book is available from the British Library.

ISBN 0 7494 0711 5

Typeset by Paul Stringer, Watford
Printed and bound in Great Britain by
Biddles Ltd, Guildford and King's Lynn

Contents

Series Editor's Foreword Chris Bell   7

Introduction   9

1. Diagrams and Learning   11
    Uses of diagrams in instruction 11
    Some characteristics of diagrams 12
    Advantages and disadvantages of diagrams 17
    Diagram design considerations 20
    Ways instructional diagrams can fail 21

2. Diagrams and Visual Literacy   23
    How diagrams are processed 23
    Visual literacy 24
    The diagram processing task 25
    How diagrams present information 26
    Importance of background knowledge 30
    Making conventions explicit 32
    Why people use diagrams poorly 34

3. The Diagram Development Process   38
    How diagrams are usually developed 38
    Dangers when including diagrams 40
    What should diagrams present? 42
    A diagram's instructional context 45

4. Designing a Diagram   47
    Graphic design versus instructional design 47
    Clarifying a diagram's instructional function 49
    Analysing the content 52
    Focusing the objectives 56
    Increasing explanatory power 59

5. Producing a Diagram — 64
Producing initial ideas 64
Developing the entities 66
Treatment of entities 70
Assembling entities into a diagram 74
Technological aids for diagram production 79

6. Instructional Diagrams in Context — 82
Visual characteristics of different media 82
Media constraints in diagram design 83
Working around media constraints 87
Computer-based diagrams 88
Animated instructional diagrams 90

7. Integrating Diagrams in Instruction — 95
Diagrams in an instructional system 95
Integrating text and diagrams 97
Complementing diagrams with text 99
Using text to guide diagram processing 100
Integrating diagrams with other resources 102

8. Improving Instructional Diagrams — 106
Approaches to evaluation 106
Learner-based evaluation 108
Learners' opinions 111
Learners' results 112
Learners' processing 114
Learners' performance 116
Gathering information 117
Field testing diagrams 119

9. Helping the Diagram User — 121
Making diagrams more manageable 121
Increasing learner involvement 122
Deeper diagram processing 124
Imagery 131

10. Conclusion — 133

Bibliography — 135

Index — 137

Series Editor's Foreword

People learn most effectively when their instruction has been designed optimally. Seemingly, this is obvious but, in practice, it is too often not the case. Whether designing for face-to-face delivery, support materials, learning media or distance independent learning, there is a need for much systematic thought, planning and evaluation.

This series is designed to help teachers and trainers apply the ideas of educational and training technology (ETT) in order to produce the most effective and efficient instruction. The books are also appropriate for people studying education and training.

'Educational and training technology', the overall theme of this series, is a much misunderstood (or not understood) phrase. In his book *The Concept of Educational Technology* (published in 1970 by Weidenfeld and Nicolson, London) Kenneth Richmond takes some 70 pages to discuss the meaning of this phrase. Numerous other authors have also spent many pages discussing the ideas from both conceptual and practical viewpoints. Definitions, often conflicting, abound.

It is my belief that the most useful way of considering ETT is to think in terms of:

- the technology *of* education and training, and
- the use of technologies *in* education and training.

The former, the less tangible, is very much a cross-disciplinary aspect, drawing on psychology, sociology, communications theory, learning theory, media research, anthropology, statistics and many more areas. The latter is much more about the applications of hardware and software to the learning process.

In both cases, the focus is on increasing the quality and efficiency of learning. ETT is concerned with the design, evaluation and assessment of the teaching/learning process (note the essential use of the term 'learning'). It is concerned with systematically analysing learning needs, and relating these to relevant theories (and none too theoretically based knowledge!) with the intention of optimizing learning. It is a rational problem-solving approach to the needs and issues of education and training; a way of thinking systematically and critically.

At its best, application of the ideas of ETT is central to the improvement of education and training, to meeting the needs of learners and to fitting the system to these needs. Together, the books in the series should help you do this, both from the perspective of the technology *of* education and training, and the use of technologies *in* education and training.

In this book, Ric Lowe takes an in-depth look at the characteristics, applications, development and evaluation of diagrams for use in instructional materials. The book approaches the subject from the perspective of someone using diagrams to facilitate their learning, whether in training or education, or in a stand-alone manner: as such, it constantly attempts to put those developing instructional diagrams 'in the shoes of the end user'.

Chris Bell

Introduction

This book is for people who wish to use diagrams to make their instructional materials more effective. It is suitable for those developing diagrams in resources ranging from advanced computer-controlled multimedia presentations to more traditional print-based resources such as textbooks. It will help instructional designers, trainers, teachers, textbook authors, desktop publishers, instructional software developers and educational technologists to take a systematic and informed approach to diagram development.

The book explains how to make diagrams an effective part of instruction by looking both at ways to improve diagram design and at strategies for helping learners to use diagrams successfully. In our visually oriented age, diagrams are increasingly seen as an essential ingredient of instructional materials. Recent advances in computer graphics mean that those without specialist design skills can now produce the artwork for diagrams quickly and easily. But will these diagrams make a worthwhile contribution to understanding and learning?

When you have finished reading this book, you will know how to use diagrams successfully in instruction. You will understand what features distinguish effective diagrams and how to support learners in their diagram processing. Further, you will be able to design and develop diagrams that function as an effective part of a wider instructional context.

1 Diagrams and Learning

Uses of diagrams in instruction

How often have you heard instructors say that 'a picture is worth a thousand words'? This statement reflects the common belief that visuals are somehow especially effective as a teaching resource. The diagram is a type of instructional visual that is widely used across many subjects, particularly those which involve technical subject matter. However, not all the diagrams found in teaching materials are equally successful in promoting the desired learning outcomes. This can be because the diagrams are so poorly designed that they actually hinder, rather than help, learning. However, even well-designed diagrams can be ineffective if the student is given insufficient support in how to use them. So, perhaps the adage about pictures could be rewritten as 'a diagram can be worth a thousand words, provided it has been well designed and is sufficiently supported'.

As with any instructional resource, the main reason for using diagrams in teaching materials is to help students learn more efficiently and effectively. In many situations this means that instructional diagrams aim to teach students how to:

- perform new tasks in an acceptable way, or
- improve the way they perform their existing tasks.

For instruction to be judged successful, the students must be able to produce the new or improved performance as required. This typically means that they need to be able to *remember* what they were taught and in many cases also carry out tasks in a way that shows they *understand* what they are doing. So, if diagrams are to be instructionally successful, they should help students to:

- recall the knowledge and skills they have been taught, and
- understand the material that is being taught.

Recall and understanding are often seen as strongly related because of the effectiveness of instruction that results in *meaningful learning*. If a diagram can help a student understand the subject matter (ie make it meaningful), recall of that material is generally likely to be better than if the instruction did not emphasize understanding.

As well as aiding recall, a good understanding of the subject matter can support problem solving and transfer of learning beyond a particular instructional context. For these reasons, this book focuses upon the use of diagrams to develop understanding.

Some characteristics of diagrams

Although so far we have not distinguished between diagrams and other forms of pictures found in teaching/learning resources, diagrams are actually quite special. Some comparisons with other sorts of pictures will help make this clearer.

In the floral depiction in Figure 1.1, the flower looks much the same as it would in real life. The reasons that it looks quite realistic include the 'natural' arrangement of its parts and their smooth, graduated shading which gives the flower a three-dimensional quality. Contrast this with the second picture (Figure 1.2) in which flowers, leaves and stems are depicted in a heavily altered form. This turns them into a decoration in which these parts of the plant are treated as elements of a stylized pattern.

Because of their overall style and treatment of the subject matter, neither the realistic nor the decorative picture could be considered to be a diagram. However, the third representation (Figure 1.3) is immediately recognizable as a diagram, even if you are not completely clear about its meaning. Its overall style is an instant giveaway, despite the fact that it has none of the labels that are characteristic of most diagrams. Straight away we are aware of the fact that it is a two-dimensional line drawing carried out in a very formal and precise manner. On closer

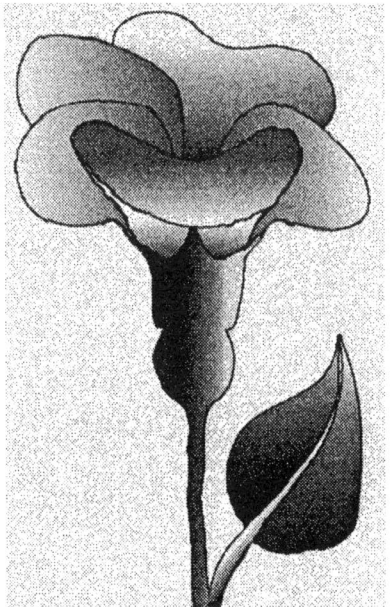

Figure 1.1 *Realistic depiction of a flower. Shapes and shading give this picture a three-dimensional appearance which makes it resemble closely what we would expect to see in real life.*

Figure 1.2 *Decorative floral arrangement. Although the depiction involves some heavy transformation of flower forms, the purpose of this stylization is aesthetic, not explanatory.*

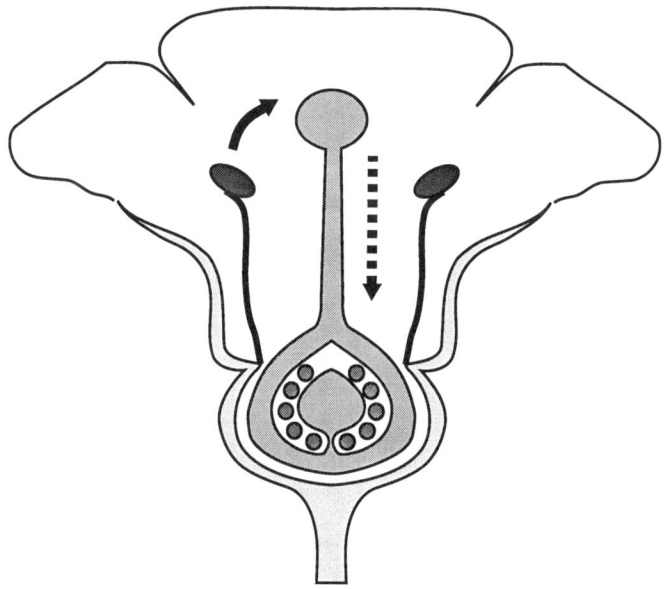

Figure 1.3 *Diagram of a flower showing reproductive parts. Transformations are used to expose and make clear the internal structure of the flower giving greater explanatory power.*

inspection, we may see it is actually a cross-section through a flower (definitely nothing like the flower's natural appearance) that reveals its internal reproductive parts. The diagram uses a variety of transformations which change the flower so it no longer looks realistic. These transformations include slicing it in half to show what's inside and simplifying many of its features. Shading and arrows have been added to help clarify the subject matter.

The aim of the third depiction is quite different from that of the previous two. It is intended to *explain* some things about the flower, in particular:

- the *structure* of the flower (the physical features of its parts and how they are arranged in space), and
- the *process* of reproduction (the changes that its parts are involved in over time).

Presenting new information about structure and processes is a common function of diagrams. We will return to these functions in more detail later in this book when we look at procedures for designing diagrams (Chapters 3, 4 and 5).

For now, we will concentrate on a specific diagram to highlight a number of important general characteristics of diagrams. This diagram (Figure 1.4) depicts the *structure* of a pepper mill used to grind peppercorns (a *process* diagram for this device will be presented later in Figure 4.2). We have chosen this particular subject matter simply because it is both a familiar household item and also gives us plenty of scope for explaining how diagrams work. (Many other types of content would have done equally well.)

With this diagram we will go some way further than just being able to recognize that it is a diagram (as we did with Figure 1.3, the third depiction of the flower). We will examine how it divides information between graphic material and associated text. Note that in the discussion that follows, the text we will consider is limited to that contained in the diagram's immediate labels and captions. For the present, we will not include more distant references to the diagram that may occur in the main body of a text in which the diagram is embedded. Ideally, the diagram's graphical and textual information should work together to help the student build up an appropriate understanding of the diagram as a whole.

The graphic components in the pepper mill diagram let us know such things as:

- what the various parts of the depicted object (pepper mill) *look like* (eg shape and size)
- where parts are *located* (eg at the top or bottom of the mill)
- which parts are *attached* or *not attached* (eg the handle is attached to the shaft but the toothed wheel is free to turn inside the grinding compartment)
- *how* parts are attached (eg the shaft is attached to the handle via a mounting and a knob).

The text lets us know:

- the *identity* of the object's components (eg the handle and the shaft)

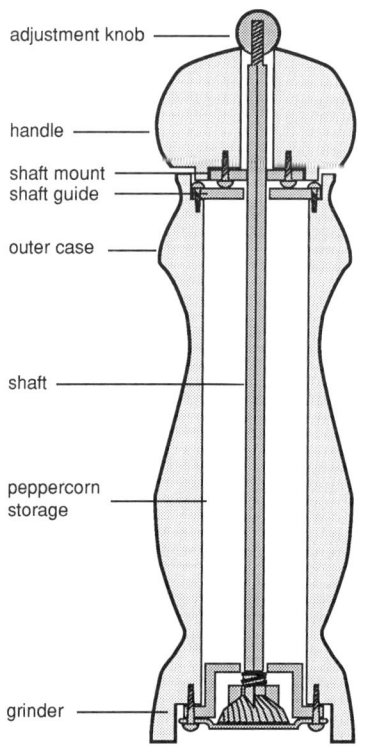
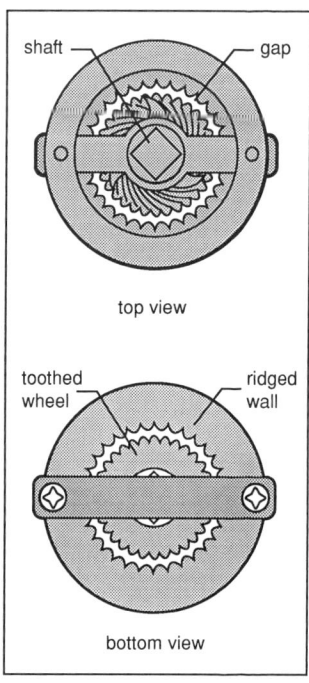

(a) **Cross section of pepper mill.** The toothed wheel in the grinder at the base of the mill is fixed to the handle at the top.

(b) **Enlarged views of grinder.** The toothed wheel is free to rotate inside the fixed ridged grinding compartment. There is a gap between the toothed wheel and the wall of the grinding compartment.

Figure 1.4 *Structure diagram of a pepper mill. Shows the physical features of the mill's parts and the way they are arranged in space. This diagram uses a composite of different views for clarity.*

- what *view* of the object we are looking at (cross-section, top or bottom view)
- how the object is *structured* (eg the handle and the toothed wheel of the grinder are connected by the shaft).

Notice how some of the information is repeated in that it is given in the form of both graphics and text. This is described as *redundant* encoding of information and can be a useful way to draw attention to what is of particular significance in a diagram. Other information is provided in only one of these forms and this is described as *non-redundant* encoding. This pattern of encoding can indicate highly visual or verbal material that is difficult to present effectively in an alternative format.

Notice also that although many of these types of information may be relevant to the way a pepper mill works, this is not a *process* diagram. It is intended to depict only the structure of the mill, not the sequence of events that takes place when peppercorns are ground into fragments. This distinction between structure and process is an important aspect of diagram design since it is often best to use different approaches for these two types of diagram.

Advantages and disadvantages of diagrams

The diagram of a pepper mill in Figure 1.4 contains some general features of diagrams that can either help or hinder learning, depending on the instructional situation (who is being taught, how the instruction is presented, what other materials accompany the diagram, etc). Typically, instructors focus upon the instructional *advantages* of diagrams without paying too much attention to the challenges that diagrams may present to the learner. For diagrams to be a successful part of instruction, a more even-handed consideration of their pros and cons is needed. Let's see how this could be done for the pepper mill diagram.

Some of the potential instructional *advantages* of this diagram arise from:

- simplifying the subject matter by reducing it from a three-dimensional to a two-dimensional depiction so that the way parts of the pepper mill are arranged becomes easier to see;
- removing unnecessary detail that is present in the real object but which has no significance in terms of its overall structure (eg the wood grain pattern on the timber case);

- enlarging parts of the object to make their features clearer (eg the grinder section of the mill to show the nature of the surfaces that grind the peppercorns);
- providing a variety of revealing views of the subject matter that expose important parts of the structure (eg cross-sectional view, top view, bottom view);
- coding conceptually different regions of the structure with a limited number of characteristic types of shading to signal their nature (dark grey is for the metal components which comprise parts of the milling mechanism, light grey is for the wooden case, white is for a space or cavity). This makes it easier to identify different aspects of the structure;
- arranging related pieces of information in close proximity to encourage those pieces to be treated together in the interpretation of the diagram (eg the top and bottom views of the grinder grouped together inside the boxed area).

However, there are also potential *disadvantages* in using diagrams, particularly with students who are not adept in making the most of these resources. Possible problems that could arise with the pepper mill diagram include the following.

- Students who are uneasy with abstract, technical representations could be 'put off' by the style of depiction. They may be more at ease initially with a more realistic picture of the object.
- Some aspects of the object depicted are less easy to identify than if a realistic depiction had been used because of the extensive transformation they have undergone.
- Reducing the representation from three to two dimensions in the name of simplification inevitably throws away spatial information which may be crucial to a proper understanding of the object's structure.
- Students who are unused to dealing with diagrams in general may approach the diagram 'literally', in other words as if it actually showed what the subject matter looked like. Because diagrams are such highly transformed representations of reality, special ways of looking at them and thinking about them are usually required.

- Providing a number of different views of the object generally requires the student to put these views together mentally in order to develop a coherent idea of what the object is like as a whole. This may be a taxing task for those who lack specific skills in the forms of mental manipulation required.
- As well as appropriately linking together the various graphic components of the diagram, students also need to integrate these components with the textual information in the captions and labels. This involves coordination of scattered items of information that must be drawn together to form a coherent whole.

After looking at this list of possible disadvantages (which is by no means complete), you may start to wonder why diagrams are used so extensively in instructional materials. Of course, in most situations, the diagram is not the only source of information available to the learner. In the case of this pepper mill, most people have some real life experience of the object. This background knowledge helps them fill in most of the information gaps that inevitably occur when subject matter is represented in diagrammatic form. So, for material that is familiar, some of the problems with diagrams mentioned above may not occur.

However, instruction is often addressed to learners who are (virtually by definition) not familiar with the subject matter. In addition, as already mentioned, they may not be skilled in the types of mental approaches and operations necessary to build up an appropriate meaning from diagrammatic representations.

These deficiencies in knowledge and skills should be considered when developing materials that will involve diagrams. Some learners may need to be given considerable support to help them deal with diagrams presented during instruction. It can be a mistake for instructional designers to treat diagrams as if they are self explanatory. This mistake is particularly unfortunate when diagrams are used as a substitute for text on the assumption that poor readers will be better able to handle information in diagrammatic form. 'Reading' abstract diagrams is a task that can be just as specialized and demanding as reading text. Chapter 9 examines some ways of providing students with support in using diagrams effectively as tools for learning.

Diagram design considerations

There are three important questions that the designer of an instructional diagram needs to consider during the design process.

1. *Who is the diagram for?*

The preceding section suggests that a diagram which is effective for one person may not be effective for another. For example, a very minimal diagram that is easily read by a teacher or advanced learner of a particular subject area may be a complete mystery to a beginning learner. Because the individual characteristics of the person who is to use the diagram play such a large part in its success, designers of instructional diagrams need to know quite a lot about who will be using the diagram.

2. *What is the **instructional purpose** of the diagram?*

We saw earlier that two important (but different) purposes of diagrams are to depict a *structure* (such as the parts of a pepper mill and their arrangement) and to depict a *process* (such as the way the pepper mill performs its grinding function). A well-designed instructional diagram will have a clear focus as to which of these purposes (or some other purpose) it is addressing, rather than trying to fulfil many purposes at once. In addition, the function of the diagram will be derived from well-defined instructional objectives, rather than being inserted as a space filler, a motivational decoration, or because 'we always use this sort of diagram in this part of the course'.

3. *What is the **situation** in which the diagram will be used?*

Diagrams are used in a wide range of instructional situations ranging from one-to-one teaching (in which there are rich opportunities for intensive, two-way interaction between instructor and learner) to isolated open learning environments (in which the learner may have no opportunity for interaction with what is essentially a stand-alone set of instructional materials). Clearly a learner in the second of these situations will face different challenges in understanding a diagram from a learner in the first. This means that when instructional materials are intended to be stand-alone resources, more support and guidance needs to be given to learners in how to use a diagram in the most instructionally effective way.

Notice that none of the above points deals with the *graphic design* aspects of the diagram *per se*. This is not to say that these design aspects are unimportant, merely to indicate that there are much more fundamental issues to be addressed before becoming involved in drafting the graphic material itself. In fact, there will be graphic design consequences that arise from each of the above considerations. For example, a less abstract graphic treatment might be used with a group of learners who were beginners in the subject area, or a structure diagram may emphasize the physical characteristics of the subject matter more than would be the case in a process diagram.

Ways instructional diagrams can fail

Too often, instructional diagrams are developed in a vacuum. They are typically the result of collaboration between a person with subject matter expertise and someone with graphic design skills. When diagrams produced by such collaboration *are* instructionally sucessful, it is likely to be a result of the ingenuity and intuition of those involved, rather than of a systematic, informed approach to diagram development. Those involved are able to make reasonable guesses about the nature of the target learners and create effective ways to represent the subject matter for those learners.

However, it can be very difficult for those who know a lot about a subject area to appreciate the position of a novice in their field. A diagram that to the subject matter expert is a perfectly clear and simple presentation of key information can be quite meaningless to someone just starting to learn about the subject. When subject matter experts have their rough drafts converted into professionally finished pieces of artwork, the people drawing up the final versions may not be able or willing to address the matter of how easy the diagrams will be for the intended audiences to understand.

Often missing from the process of developing diagrams is someone who looks at the instructional situation as a whole. An instructional design specialist with particular expertise in how instructional diagrams fit into this larger situation can fulfil this role by asking questions such as the following.

- What are the characteristics of the target learners for whom the diagram is being developed?
- What do the target learners see as being the role of the diagram in performing the learning task and how does this influence the way they use the diagram?
- What role is given to the diagram by its designers in helping the target learners carry out a particular learning task?
- How are the diagram and its accompanying text related to each other?
- What assumptions are made about how target learners will need to interact with the diagram and its associated text?
- To what extent and in what way do the target learners actually use the diagram during their study?

During the course of this book, we will show you how to find answers to these and related questions. This approach will help you to design and use diagrams in ways that are instructionally successful.

2 Diagrams and Visual Literacy

How diagrams are processed

In designing an instructional diagram, it is important to know as much as possible about what the students might 'do' with that diagram when they come across it in an instructional resource. We can think of a diagram as a tool for learning. It is a tool that students can use in their minds to carry out the thinking processes required to perform particular learning tasks. Like any tool, a diagram's effectiveness depends on how well it is used by its 'operator' (the person viewing the diagram). Even the best-designed instructional diagram imaginable can only be effective if students use it properly.

If the viewer does not process a diagram effectively in his or her mind, the diagram cannot perform the function its designer intended. For the diagram to be successful, the viewer needs to process it in such a way that the end result built up in his or her mind closely matches the author's intentions. If a viewer processes a diagram in an *inappropriate* way, the result can be an 'understanding' of the diagram that was *not* intended by the author (such as a very superficial understanding or a serious misunderstanding of the subject matter). But sometimes a particular viewer may find a specific diagram quite impenetrable and not even know how to *begin* processing it. We could say that as far as this person is concerned, the meaning of such a diagram is 'opaque'.

In this chapter, we will focus upon what demands diagram *processing* makes on the viewer. This will help to explain why a viewer can still fail to use a diagram effectively, even when the diagram itself has no major design faults.

Visual literacy

Although the concept of literacy is normally associated with text, it can be extended to include pictorial materials as in the notion of *'visual* literacy'. We will use this notion when discussing diagram processing.

It is accepted that to learn from text, a person needs a level and type of literacy appropriate to the nature of the text to be read. In addition to a sufficient command of written language in general, a reader also needs to be skilled in the specialized genre of writing that characterizes the particular subject area being presented. For example, the way language is used in a technical training manual is not the same as it is used in a history text. Just because a person can read a history text, we cannot assume that person can read a technical training manual effectively.

Literacy in visual modes of presentation can be seen in some situations as just as fundamental to learning as literacy with respect to written text. Visual literacy includes the capacity to 'read' visual displays effectively. However, the idea that visual literacy is necessary for reading visual materials is not as widely accepted as the self-evident fact that textual literacy is required for reading text. This is partly because visual materials in general are typically not considered to pose any reading challenges to the viewer. In contrast to text, their meaning is assumed to be 'transparent' (which explains why many regard visuals as *solutions* to instructional problems, especially for those who have difficulty in learning from text).

However, it is unwise to treat all visual materials as if they were equally accessible to the viewer. In particular, diagrams need to be considered as a special case because they have some characteristics that are quite unlike most other types of visual material. Diagrams are not like 'other pictures' and so require the reader to have specific *diagram knowledge* and *diagram reading skills* that are not required for most of the pictures we encounter. So, a person who is visually literate with respect to the usual types of visual materials we meet in our everyday lives may not be visually literate with respect to diagrams.

Given, then, that there is a specialized form of visual literacy that pertains to diagrams, what does this mean if our goal is to maximize the effectiveness of diagrams as aids to instruction? We should not assume that all readers will possess the knowledge and skills required to use diagrams effectively as a learning tool. This would mean that, to be an effective part of a learning resource, a diagram may have to be accompanied by supporting material that helps the readers process it properly. This issue will be discussed further later in the book.

The diagram processing task

The job facing the viewer of a diagram is a bit like that faced by an archaeologist who finds a few scattered remains of an ancient city. How does the archaeologist try to work out what the city must have been like originally? It probably happens something like this. The archaeologist blends the very limited *external* physical evidence from the visible remains with rich *internal* knowledge (that is stored inside his or her head) about ancient cities and how to interpret their remains. In a similar way, the viewer of a diagram inevitably makes a major contribution to its effectiveness because understanding is constructed partly from the external information in the diagram and partly from internal information within the viewer's head.

When students are presented with incomplete information, they try to fill the gaps in that information using knowledge they have stored in memory. In one respect, a good diagram is an incomplete set of information. This is because, when the diagram is being developed, anything considered not of immediate and central relevance to the subject matter is removed. Unlike the remains in an archaeological site, the missing material is removed with the specific aim of making the subject matter clearer. This removal is carried out deliberately in a structured, systematic and highly conventionalized way. So, to interpret properly the set of markings that makes up a particular diagram, the viewer needs to be able to 'reconstruct' the situation it depicts. We can think of this as being something like the way an archaeologist reconstructs the appearance of an ancient city from its remains. However, if the learner is unable to perform this reconstruction properly, the diagram can remain shrouded in mystery rather than acting to clarify the subject matter.

What does a viewer need to do in order to carry out this diagram reconstruction process effectively? This question is at the heart of making sense of a diagram in order to learn about its subject matter. We have already had some clues. Essentially, there are two major requirements:

- identifying all the relevant information in the diagram and realizing its significance in the context concerned;
- adding to this diagram information, whatever else is needed to build up a full representation of the depicted situation in the viewer's mind (using prior knowledge to fill gaps in the evidence).

These requirements are both related to the way that diagrams present information.

How diagrams present information

In Chapter 1 we saw that it was quite easy to recognize diagrams and distinguish them from other forms of depiction (such as realistic pictures and decorative graphics) because of their overall appearance. However, when trying to *design* effective instructional diagrams or decide how to help learners *make best use* of them, we need to go further than these overall impressions. We need to consider how a diagram's individual characteristics (which together contribute to its overall appearance) are meant to convey information.

Diagrams use a host of particular devices and techniques to help them present the subject matter. These devices and techniques have been developed to give diagrams the power to present and explain in ways that can make them instructionally superior to more literal ('realistic') depictions. Instead of presenting the content in a manner that is faithful (in a graphic sense) to the original, diagrams intentionally distort or completely alter various aspects of reality. For example, they greatly simplify the material presented by leaving many things out of the depiction and reorganizing what little is retained. As well as *omitting* much normally visible material, they also *add* a range of graphic markings (such as arrows) that do not represent visible material but which can make the explanation clearer.

However, while these transformations of the subject matter are intended to help make the presentation clearer and the explanation more effective, they can also pose challenges for some learners. It is useful to compare diagrams with both text and realistic pictures to see how these challenges might arise. An understanding of these potential challenges to the learner can help make the diagram designer more aware of some of the possible pitfalls in the design process.

Diagrams versus text

In normal reading, people move through a block of text in a quite regular way for most of the time. For example, with most European languages, there is a general left-to-right, top-to-bottom exploration that works through the information in a fairly predictable sequential manner.

As they progress through a piece of text, readers can make use of a variety of textual 'signposts' along the way that help them to:

- gauge the *significance* of what they are reading, and
- understand the *overall structure* of the information presented.

These signposts include punctuation, headings and sub-headings, forms of emphasis such as bold face or italic type and the way space is used on the page. The way text uses these aids to the reader is highly conventionalized and governed to a large extent by formal or informal rules that competent readers typically utilize without conscious effort.

Although vocabulary and style of writing vary according to the subject matter, the more general conventions referred to above remain. Even the larger forms of organization found in written text are fairly consistent across different types of subject matter. For example, most textbooks will start with a list of contents, have their content organized by chapters, then end with sections such as an index and a glossary. Within each of these major subdivisions, the material will generally be arranged in a standard format. Frequently, the reader will be given explicit guidance as to the intentions of the book and how best to approach its reading.

All of the regularities and conventions mentioned here for text are a great help for readers. They let readers know what to expect and what is an appropriate way to tackle the task of building up a coherent meaning from the information presented in a book. For example, they know that it is probably a good idea to work more or less sequentially through the book or a particular block of text within that book (although there are exceptions).

The process of reading text involves readers in putting together the information presented *on the page* (external) with the knowledge they already possess *inside their heads* (internal). In this respect, it also resembles the previous description of how an archaeologist mentally reconstructs the original situation from an ancient ruin. Two important types of internal knowledge that help a reader use text effectively are:

- knowledge about the world in general and the subject matter of the text in particular
- knowledge about how text works as a means of presenting information and the way it should be processed for best effect.

So, how might reading a diagram differ from reading text? We say 'might' because so far there has been much less research into how people process diagrams than there has been for text processing. This means that much of the discussion to follow is based upon more general research, application of learning principles, analysis of the different demands that appear to be imposed by diagrams, and practical experience. However, where relevant research has been carried out with diagrams and similar materials, the findings have been used.

Diagrams do not have the same degree of standardization as text. We have seen that it is usually quite easy to recognize that a particular depiction is a diagram rather than some other type of picture. However, it is not so easy to find the same types of regularities among diagrams that can be found among texts.

Despite the informality of many of the rules governing text and its various levels of organization, these rules are still generally well known by a wide cross-section of people. Even if many competent readers are unable to state these rules explicitly or are only dimly aware of a text's organization, they are still able to *make use* of the rules and organization to help them read effectively.

In contrast, diagrams vary greatly in both the types of graphic elements from which they are comprised and in the organizational conventions that are involved in assembling these elements. The 'rules' are much less clear (if indeed we can really call them rules). This means that some learners will not know nearly as much about how to use diagrams and how they should be processed as they would know about text. You may have met people who say that they ignore the diagrams when reading a textbook because they find them difficult to understand. One task that can face the designer of instructional diagrams is to address this reluctance of some people even to *engage* with the diagrams provided.

As well as facing the challenge of *unfamiliar subject matter*, learners who do not routinely use diagrams as learning tools (or who have never encountered a particular, specialized type of diagram) may also be hampered by their *lack of diagram knowledge*.

Diagrams versus other pictures

Ordinary, everyday pictures usually show their subject matter in much the same way as we might expect to see them in real life. There is a realistic portrayal of both the things (*entities*) that make up the subject matter and the way that these entities are organized. One way to describe this type of representation is to say that there is a fairly direct mapping of the subject matter into the depiction. Although this realistic type of portrayal allows us to recognize the objects and situations readily, it does limit the power of such pictures to provide *explanations*. For example, if you saw a photograph of a pepper mill, it would be very easy to tell what it was and to appreciate its overall structure. However, such a depiction would tell you little about the functional components of the mill and essentially nothing about the way these components grind peppercorns into pepper.

When people look at ordinary pictures, they generally expect objects to look the way they do in everyday life. However, this is often not a reasonable expectation for diagrams. As a consequence, the graphic material that makes up a diagram needs to be approached and processed very differently from the graphic material we find in ordinary pictures.

Importance of background knowledge

What a person sees and understands when viewing a diagram very much depends upon what s/he is primed to see. Part of this priming is provided by the immediate instructional setting in which the diagram is encountered. This *external* context includes the particular learning task that the viewer is asked to undertake with the diagram. However, another important influence on diagram processing is what the viewer brings to the task in the form of mental priming due to prior knowledge. This *internal* priming relies on what the viewer already knows about such things as the:

- subject matter depicted in the diagram
- wider context in which that subject matter occurs
- graphic treatment used to depict the subject matter
- conventions that must be taken into account when interpreting the diagram's constituents
- significance and relative importance of the different types of material that constitute the diagram
- overall organization of the diagram
- relationships that are likely to be present among the diagram's constituents
- usual exploration pattern that a viewer would be expected to follow in reading such a diagram.

Although these aspects of prior knowledge will be addressed in more detail later in this book, let us for now illustrate just a few ways in which they may influence a person's capacity to make effective use of a diagram. At a fundamental level, the viewer needs to be able to recognize the graphic entities which make up the diagram. This is rather like saying that a person reading text needs to be able to recognize the words encountered. So we can think of these graphic entities as the *vocabulary* of the diagram. Sometimes this vocabulary is made up of special symbols instead of shapes that resemble the things represented in the diagram. For example, an electronic circuit diagram uses abstract symbols whose identity must be known before the diagram can be understood.

However, this type of background knowledge about vocabulary alone is not sufficient to produce understanding. The viewer also needs to know some of the real-life *characteristics* of the things that are represented in the diagram. For example, the different symbols in an electronic circuit diagram stand for electronic components that have different effects on electricity. Some components allow the electric current to be turned on or off completely while some have other effects such as limiting or controlling the current. Further, these components do not exist in isolation but are connected to form various arrangements that have a larger-scale effect on the electric current. So the viewer also needs to be able to interpret the graphic *relationships* shown on the diagram as real-life relationships that have an effect over and above the effects of individual components.

This example of an electronic circuit diagram highlights the fact that, in some circumstances, the instructional designer may be dealing with a well-established diagram format. For such diagrams, the nature of the symbols and how these symbols are to be used are largely predetermined due to a high degree of standardization. So the components and structure of an electronic circuit diagram cannot be manipulated to any great extent by an instructional designer in an effort to 'improve' the depiction. Other than developing additions to the basic diagram that help to clarify what is represented, the instructional designer's role is necessarily restricted to providing other forms of support for the viewer. However, this support can be quite critical in determining the ultimate instructional effectiveness of the diagram. In this situation, the designer's task may be to help the learner understand electronic circuit diagrams as a means to the eventual end of using these circuit diagrams to learn about electronics. However, even with many less-standardized diagrams in which the designer has had considerable freedom in devising the representation, thought often also needs to be given to teaching the learner how to read the diagram.

Making conventions explicit

One source of difficulty that learners can have with diagrams comes about because of the conventions used, many of which change from diagram to diagram. So, while some diagram conventions are quite formal and well-defined, many others are much looser and less standardized. There is certainly nothing like the widespread agreement that exists in the use of text conventions.

The designer of diagrams needs to consider the influence of these conventions both at the stage of constructing a diagram ('the designer's end') and at the stage of reading the diagram ('the viewer's end'). Some conventions apply to the way the subject matter is depicted while others apply to the way it is intended to be interpreted. So a designer may adopt the widespread diagram depictive convention of using a two-dimensional line drawing and then add a particular level of shading to indicate parts of the subject matter that the viewer needs to interpret as conceptually related.

Often, subject matter experts are not aware of the potential problems that diagram conventions can cause because these conventions are second nature to such experts. They have no need to deal with them in a conscious manner. However, for those who are meeting these conventions for the first time, their meaning and significance may not be at all clear. So for *instructional* diagrams (as opposed to those intended for people who are already well-versed in the subject area), it is usually wise to address conventions explicitly. The diagram designer should question the subject matter expert closely about each of the conventions used to ensure that the meaning is precise. In addition, the designer should also be on the lookout for any potential sources of ambiguity or confusion in the way the conventions are used.

There are various ways to inform the viewer about the conventions used in a diagram including:

- direct labelling (annotations) of the purpose and interpretation of graphic material on the diagram itself
- the use of explanatory keys set away from the main body of the diagram
- explanation in the accompanying text (with or without graphic elements set into the textual discussion)
- provision of a preliminary supplementary diagram that has the sole role of explaining the conventions to be used on the main diagram.

Each of these methods has particular strengths and weaknesses that should be considered before adoption. For example, the direct labelling of graphic material could result in such a cluttered arrangement that the original simplicity of a diagram was compromised. In addition, there is a danger that the processes used to inform the viewer about the conventions will intrude upon the central explanatory purpose of the diagram itself. So, considerable judgement is needed in providing the viewer with support.

Especially confusing for beginners in a subject is the use of the same graphic entity for different purposes without any explanation being offered about the change of interpretation required. This can be illustrated very effectively with the inconsistent use of arrows. Because arrows have such a range of potential uses in instructional diagrams, they need to be used with particular care. Where possible, it is better to try and avoid using arrows with different meanings within the same diagram. If it is absolutely necessary to use arrows for different functions, it is important to:

- give the functionally different types of arrows physical appearances that are clearly very different; and
- provide the reader with support in precisely how to interpret each of these arrow types.

Why people use diagrams poorly

At the beginning of this chapter, we saw that good design alone is no guarantee that people will use a diagram effectively as a resource for learning. We will conclude the chapter by looking at some of the ways in which a well-designed instructional diagram can be poorly used by learners. In this discussion, we will not deal specifically with failures that arise from a lack of subject matter knowledge or knowledge of the graphic vocabulary used in the diagram. Rather, we will concentrate on poor diagram use that stems largely from inappropriate forms of processing. Let's assume a reasonably favourable situation in which we have well motivated learners who during their learning activities make at least some use of the diagrams provided in an instructional resource. Their use of the diagrams could nevertheless be instructionally inadequate for reasons that include the following types of failure.

1. Lack of 'effort' (under-rating the demands of diagram processing)
Although many everyday pictures can be interpreted perfectly adequately with little more than a casual glance, diagrams typically require far more careful analysis. Because part of the process of developing a diagram is to strip away all inessential information, it follows that everything that remains is potentially significant. As a result, diagrams usually need to be explored in a detailed and systematic manner so that no key pieces of information are overlooked. If learners who are unused to dealing with diagrams apply the same informal approaches to diagrams as they do to more everyday illustrations, they are unlikely to process the diagrams appropriately.

2. Misplaced effort Learners can process a diagram in a variety of ways, some of which may not lead to the result anticipated by the designers of the instruction. Examples of misplaced effort include the following.

- Adopting a rote-learning approach to memorizing the diagram by processing it in terms of its superficial graphic characteristics, that is:

(a) the *visual* properties of its graphic entities, such as their sizes, shapes and rendering, and

(b) the *spatial* arrangement of these graphic entities.

While this approach may allow the learner to recall the graphic pattern that made up the diagram, it is unlikely to promote an understanding of the subject matter that the diagram was meant to represent.

- Not knowing where to start or how to work systematically through the diagram. If the type of diagram is quite unfamiliar to the learners or rather complex, they may have no idea how to 'get their foot in the door' and begin productive processing. This is not a case of taking a casual approach to the diagram, simply one of being unable to initiate a productive strategy for exploring it in an appropriate way. Diagrams need to be interrogated rather than viewed and to carry out this interrogation effectively, learners may need help in asking the right series of questions.
- Taking the material in the diagram 'literally' rather than expecting it to be a highly transformed version of the situation it represents. The chances are that a diagram will bear little resemblance to the natural state of its subject matter, so learners need to expect the unusual. If learners fail to realize that what they are looking at probably incorporates all sorts of transformations, they will be unprepared to 'reverse' these transformations mentally as needed during the interpretation process.
- Focusing on one level of meaning of a diagram while ignoring the possibility of others. It may be that a diagram has a broad overarching structure that subsumes progressively more detailed levels of meaning. For example, in broad terms, all domestic pepper mills have the same overarching structure (a cavity to store the peppercorns, a grinder to break the peppercorns into fragments, and a handle with which to turn the grinder). These high-level features are common to all models, despite their considerable individual variation at the more detailed level. To deal with diagrams conceptually, the learner needs to able to incorporate a multilevel approach to processing (ranging from local to global). In many diagrams, it is productive to make several

'passes' across the diagram, perhaps beginning in a very general way to work out its overall organization and then progressively breaking the diagram down at a more detailed level.
- Failing to pick up processing clues. Many diagrams use a variety of devices to guide the viewer's reading and interpretation. For example, the recommended reading sequence may be indicated by devices such as arrows, numbers, labels or captions. The use of circles or boxes to identify key pieces of information is another example. In some cases, the cues are much less explicit, such as the adjacent placement of two similar diagrams with the intention that the learner compares them carefully in order to pick up their subtle differences. Because the way these cues are used in different diagrams can vary greatly (and are often not second nature to the learner as are the cues found in text passages), the learner needs to take a flexible approach to interpretation and regard it as a problem-solving task. If learners do not use these cues in the intended manner, much of the meaning of the diagram will be lost.
- Giving too little attention to the relations depicted within the diagram (*internal* relations). The main purpose of many diagrams (and one of the things that diagrams do best) is to depict relations. The concrete and readily accessible visual and spatial properties of diagrams are manipulated so that various graphic relations can be made to stand for a whole range of other real-world relations that would otherwise be much less tangible for the learner. However, if learners do not actively seek out these diagram relations and convert them into the real-world relations they represent, it is difficult for a diagram to serve its intended purpose. Some of these relations concern characteristics of the subject matter itself (such as using separation in space to stand for separation in time). However, others involve implicit 'instructions' to the learner to carry out certain types of processing activities on the material presented (such as the use of the same shading for different parts of the diagram that the learner is expected to relate to each other in some way).

- Failing to relate the diagram to the larger world (*external relations*). Although the learners may actually possess (or have ready access to) sufficient related background knowledge, they do not realize that they can make use of it to help them develop their understanding of the diagram. For example, by considering the occasions on which they have used pepper mills, the learners may find they have a considerable store of experience that can help them understand a pepper mill diagram. It is important for learners to realize that part of their job in trying to understand a diagram is to relate it to what they already know and so flesh out the diagrammatic representation (since the diagram is such an economical depiction).

3 The Diagram Development Process

How diagrams are usually developed

In this chapter we will assume that the diagrams for an instructional resource are to be prepared according to the established practice of employing a graphics professional to execute the finished artwork. However, with the advent of sophisticated graphics computer software it is becoming increasingly possible for authors to carry out all stages of the diagram development process themselves, including this final stage.

In Chapter 1, the point was made that the diagrams used in instructional materials are often developed by a collaboration between a subject matter expert and a person whose expertise lies in graphic design. A typical series of events in such a collaboration might be as follows:

1. The subject matter expert who is the author of the instructional materials develops the main body of the instruction (usually as some form of written text, although it could be a flow chart, series of storyboards, etc). Whatever its particular form, we will refer to it as a 'manuscript'. As part of this development, instructions concerning diagrams to accompany the manuscript are produced. The form of these instructions specifying the artwork may include:
   - roughs drawn up by the author
   - examples of diagrams from other sources that indicate the type of diagram required (often with annotations regarding modifications that the author wishes to incorporate)
   - other forms of artwork (such as photographs) from which diagrams are to be prepared

- detailed written descriptions that specifically set out the contents of the diagrams
- brief descriptions of the general type of diagram to be developed
- a request for a suitable diagram to be developed to illustrate a nominated section of the author's text.

2. The artwork specifications (sometimes with parts or the whole of the accompanying manuscript) are given to the artist(s) who then prepares a set of roughs or drafts for the diagrams. There may or may not be direct consultation with the author during this process. Indeed, in some situations, a formal separation is maintained between author and artist.

3. The artwork goes through one or more drafts with the author and artist interacting (often at a distance) until there is a satisfactory result. During this interaction, any errors of fact with respect to the subject matter will be detected by the author, and the artist will refine the diagram so that the desired result is produced.

Because the development of artwork in this way is a relatively time-consuming (and thus expensive) process, the author should try to be as specific as possible about the required diagram. It is a good idea to present information about what is needed for each diagram in a number of formats. Some formats can act as pictorial reference material for the artwork while others can help the artist understand what the diagram is meant to do for the learner.

Vague limited descriptions can be difficult to turn into acceptable diagrams, causing frustration for both the author and the artist. Such ill-defined 'specifications' often result in the poor practice of sending the same piece of artwork back over and over again for multiple modifications that are really a result of the author gradually working out his or her ideas. The author should therefore have his or her ideas very clearly worked out *before* they are presented to the artist. It is a mistake to assume that someone whose expertise is in producing visuals with a professional appearance can be left do all the conceptual and instructional thinking that should have been done before the specification was presented.

However, while the author needs to have done his or her 'homework' before presenting the specifications to the graphics designer, care should be taken not to be too prescriptive about the graphic aspects which are not fundamental to the instructional effectiveness of the diagram. Most artists engaged in this type of work have a wealth of experience and visual creativity that can enhance the diagram dramatically. As long as the author makes it clear to the artist *what* the diagram should be trying to do and *why*, the artist's expertise can be utilized in an effective manner to produce diagrams that are of a high standard both graphically and instructionally.

Many of the difficulties which occur in this situation can be circumvented if an instructional designer who is well versed in what is required to develop diagrams that are instructionally effective is involved in the above process. Where this is not possible, the author should become thoroughly acquainted with what is required to develop instructionally successful diagrams.

Dangers when including diagrams

There is a mixture of reasons why illustrations such as diagrams are used in instructional materials. Some of these reasons are the result of clearly thought out and highly specific instructional analysis. However, other reasons may be less well defined or else motivated by concerns that are not central to instruction and so contain potential traps for the diagram development process. Consider the following reasons for including diagrams in an instructional resource and decide how important you think each one is to the effectiveness of that resource. Can you see any dangers in accepting reasons such as these as the *main* justification for including diagrams?

- Learners are motivated in a general sort of way by the use of pictorial material because it provides relief in breaking up the text and students find pictures more 'approachable' than text.

- Pictorial material is an instructional medium that is inherently more effective than text – it simply explains things better or is intrinsically more memorable.
- Today's learners live in a highly visually oriented world and so are especially well 'attuned' to processing information in pictorial format.
- Instructional materials above all must first capture and maintain the attention of the learner. It is well known that visual forms of presentation are highly effective in this regard.
- Pictorial presentation provides learners who have trouble learning from text with an alternative means of access to the subject matter.
- Instructional resources that include a healthy amount of pictorial material are more likely to produce good sales figures than those that are largely text based.

If the *only* reasons for using diagrams are similar to those given above, some serious rethinking needs to be done. Although some of them hold more than a grain of truth, others are either highly speculative or else much too simplistic. Reasons such as these are useful to consider but by themselves they ignore some quite fundamental aspects of what learning resources should do for the learner. Like any other component of an instructional resource, each diagram must 'pull its weight' in terms of making a worthwhile contribution to learning.

We already expect the *text* in a textbook to assist the learner in an efficient manner. It must be well focused on the topic, carefully constructed to explain the material clearly to the intended audience, and written so that there are no wasted words. Similarly, we cannot afford to be muddle headed about what a diagram is supposed to contribute to learning. It is just as important to have well-defined instructional objectives for diagrams as it is for other components of instruction. It is also necessary to be very hard nosed about exactly how the diagram will function as part of the overall instructional resource. It can be a good idea to devise a *written* justification for a diagram that is to be used as part of the instruction and to have a colleague play 'devil's advocate'.

What should diagrams present?

Because diagrams are essentially very abbreviated visual summaries of their subject matter, the question of what will be included in a diagram is critical to its success. In principle, everything that is not 'essential' to the purpose of the diagram should be stripped away. Put simply, we could say, 'When in doubt, throw it out'.

People are overwhelmed if they are presented with too much information at once. A good guide is to limit the amount of information presented to between five and nine individual pieces (sometimes referred to as 'the magic number of seven plus or minus two pieces'). So, stripping things down to the bare essentials seems to make good sense.

Let's consider this approach with our pepper mill example. Suppose our concern is with the angle of the teeth on the toothed wheel in the grinding section of a pepper mill. In this case only the wheel and it's teeth need be shown. We can dispense with all the other components of the grinder. The teeth could be represented as simple angled lines (rather than trying to depict their contours) and, since all the teeth are set at the same angle, only a few of the teeth need be shown. Figure 3.1 illustrates how this might be done. Notice that only part of the toothed wheel is shown to keep the diagram as simple as possible.

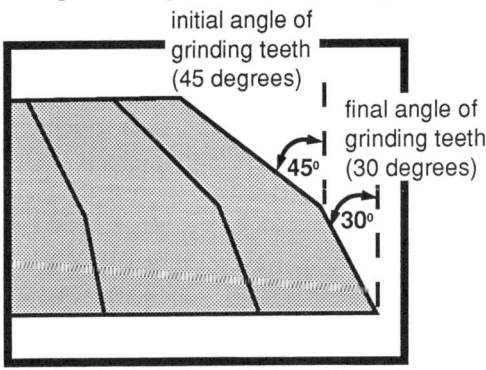

Figure 3.1 *Mill wheel grinding angles. The focus in this diagram is on the angles of the teeth on the pepper mill grinding wheel. Although the diagram is simple in graphical terms, its interpretation relies on prior knowledge.*

Although this diagram is not at all complex in *graphical* terms (since it uses just a few simple angled lines), it requires considerable sophistication in terms of the way that it is intended to be 'read'. How can it be that reading this simple diagram is such a sophisticated process? Haven't we done the right thing by reducing to a minimum the number of pieces of information the viewer has to handle?

The reason that the diagram could still be demanding is that viewers must deal with the *meaning* of the pieces of information as well as *how many* are presented. This requires the viewer to fill in a lot of informational gaps in the depiction (as was discussed in Chapter 2). Consider the following.

- The particular part of a pepper grinder that forms the subject matter of this diagram is *normally hidden* from view. The reader probably lacks prior knowledge of its appearance and so could find it difficult to relate this highly abbreviated depiction to the object it represents.
- There is *insufficient context* shown as to what larger system (the pepper grinder) this object is part of and where it is located within that system. Without clues about what the object belongs to and where it fits, it is much more difficult to determine its identity.
- Only *part* of the toothed wheel itself is shown, making it more difficult to identify even if the reader was already familiar with the real-life appearance of this part of the grinder.
- Many of the *subtle graphic characteristics* that give the toothed wheel its real-life appearance are not included. The removal of these visual clues makes the object more difficult to identify.
- The diagram has a *specialized purpose* that has little to do with the appearance of the subject matter *per se*. Instead, it is intended to isolate particular *quantitative* characteristics of the toothed wheel.
- A number of *explanatory additions* have been made to the diagram that are intended to help identify salient features of the subject matter but which require appropriate interpretation to develop the intended meaning.

The above points show that there can be an instructional price to pay in throwing away information for the sake of graphic simplicity and in adding various 'extras' to signal the information that should be attended to by the learner. So, how do we cope with the conflict between trying to obtain graphic simplicity on one hand and making the subject matter meaningful to the viewer on the other? Our task is somehow to provide the viewer with ways to make sense of the diagram without destroying the very directness that gives a simple diagram its explanatory potential.

It is a fundamental requirement that viewers can easily determine *what they are looking at* in a diagram and what they should do with it. Specifically, they must be able to work out such things as:

- the identity of the general subject matter being depicted (What's the stuff I'm looking at here?)
- the instructional purpose of the diagram (What is this diagram trying to explain to me and how am I supposed to make use of it to help me learn?)
- their viewing position relative to that subject matter (Am I looking at the top? One of the sides? The inside?)
- the focus of the diagram (Am I looking at the whole thing or only part of it? Which part am I looking at and where is it located with respect to the other parts and the external context? Why is this part of interest at the moment?)
- the ways in which the diagram differs from the real-life situation (How has the author modified the subject matter in making this diagram and so what do I have to interpret rather than take literally?)

A single diagram cannot hope to address all these aspects at once and yet retain the required simplicity. So, the solution is to treat each diagram as part of a process of *unfolding the subject matter* in the instructional resource. The instructional designer needs to relate a particular diagram to the material that precedes it, is associated with it and which follows it. In other words, a great deal of care should be given to the *context* in which each diagram is presented.

An example of this on a physical level would be to ensure that a diagram which is referred to in a passage of text is located as closely as possible to that text (preferably so that text and diagram can be studied simultaneously). An example on an instructional level would be to ensure that a close-up diagram which showed only a small part of the subject matter was preceded or accompanied by a global view showing the location and relative size of the magnified portion.

Let's apply this general idea of thinking about context to a previous diagram. Go back and have another look at Figure 3.1 for a moment. How would you 'prepare' the learners to help ensure that they understood what this diagram was all about? See how many ways you can think of to address this problem.

A diagram's instructional context

Instructional diagrams do not exist in a vacuum. They are used in a particular context of instruction and this context needs to be considered in the design process. The context exists at a number of levels which include the following.

- The immediate context of the surrounding text (or other instructional material) in which the diagram is directly situated. For example, a textual description that 'walks' the reader through the structure of the pepper mill in Figure 1.4.
- The more distant context of related material that is less directly associated with the diagram in question. For example, Figure 3.1 showing the angles of teeth on the pepper mill's toothed wheel can be considered to be set indirectly in the context of the structure diagram in Chapter 1 (Figure 1.4).
- The context of the instructional resource as a whole. For example, all the diagrams in this book are intended to serve the overall purpose of explaining aspects affecting the development of successful instructional diagrams.
- The broad context of the task and instructional setting in which the resource containing the diagram is to be used. For example, if you are an artist reading this book, you will probably be treating its diagrams somewhat differently

from the way they would be treated by an instructional designer.

Suppose the main reasons for including diagrams in an instructional resource are those such as 'breaking up pages of text' or 'competing with the learner's existing highly stimulating visual environment'. These types of reasons suggest that the instructional context of the diagram has not been given sufficiently deep consideration. It is important to put yourself in the place of the learner as fully as you can in order to characterize the context as comprehensively as possible. Go beyond treating the diagram as just another component of the instructional resource and think through the *processes* that a learner would have to carry out in order to gain full benefit from the diagram. Even better, involve typical target learners in the development process.

4 Designing a Diagram

Graphic design versus instructional design

Producers of instructional materials want those resources to 'look good', in other words to be attractive and have a professional finish. In this visual age, the quality of the artwork used to illustrate books or other materials plays an important part in:

- capturing the attention of potential users (often a marketing consideration)
- maintaining a user's interest so that s/he persists with the material.

As a result, the role of graphic design in instructional materials has become increasingly important as they move away from a largely text-based presentation toward a more visual approach. Publishers are more inclined to use fancy page layouts and eye-catching visuals, all designed to make the material more appealing. Educators often support this approach on the grounds that instructional materials must compete with the dazzling array of visual stimuli that surround learners in their everyday lives.

While gaining and holding the learner's attention is undoubtedly an important part of the instructional process, good teaching materials do far more. In particular, they help present the subject matter in a way that makes it easier for the learner to understand and remember that content. This is why it is important to distinguish between *graphic* design and *instructional* design. A designer with a high level of professional expertise in producing graphics will not necessarily be able to produce effective *instructional* graphics without considerable guidance from an instructional designer. Consider what would happen to a learner whose attention is attracted by the overall appearance (graphic design) of a particular instructional resource only to find that its diagrams were poorly designed or supported from an instructional point of view. If the diagrams are ambiguous, overwhelming, difficult to interpret or deficient with regard to some essential aspects of explanation, no amount of graphic design alone can overcome their instructional inadequacies.

In the following discussion, we assume that the finished artwork for your instructional materials will be prepared by professional artists from the rough drafts that you have developed. However, even if you will be preparing your own finished artwork by taking advantage of a computer-based drawing package, the basic distinction between graphic design and instructional design still applies.

A professional finished artist typically has expertise in designing graphics rather than in designing instruction. In presenting a draft diagram to such an artist, an author should not have unreasonable expectations about how the draft will change when reworked into a finished piece of artwork. The expected result should be that a diagram is faithful to the spirit and content of the draft with a high quality, professionally drawn appearance. It is not the artist's job to redesign the instructional aspects of the diagram any more than it is for them to alter key aspects of the subject matter to be depicted.

Most artists are careful to follow the author's draft since they usually lack the necessary specialist subject knowledge to do anything else. Similarly, they will generally assume that the instructional aspects of the diagram have also been worked out before they receive it and will not make major alterations in the way the subject matter is presented. So, if the draft is factually correct and yet instructionally inadequate, its conversion to finished form will not usually correct deficiencies in its instructional design.

Of course there are some exceptional artists who have a special flair for incorporating effective instructional characteristics into their diagram design. However, even these artists may not have access to an overview of the wider instructional situation into which the diagrams must fit. For example, it would be unusual for them to have an intimate knowledge of the text which is associated with the diagram and how the two of these are designed to form an integrated instructional whole. This remains the responsibility of the author or the instructional designer who oversees development of the materials.

So, when you present your draft to be turned into finished artwork, it is vital that it incorporates the approaches and techniques which help to make a diagram instructionally effective. Naturally, you will have an opportunity to ask for minor revisions to the diagram when you see the artwork but these should not affect its fundamental instructional design. Because artwork is one of the more expensive parts of publication, you will probably have to carry the costs of major redesign yourself.

Clarifying a diagram's instructional function

Let's suppose that we have made the general decision that a diagrammatic depiction is a suitable way to present a particular aspect of the instruction. Our next step is to tackle the specifics of the design process. The first thing to clarify is just how the diagram is meant to contribute to the instruction. In discussing some of these possible contributions, we will take it for granted that the *overall* purpose is to increase understanding and/or recall and we will focus upon some of the more specific functions that diagrams can have in facilitating instruction. It is useful to structure the discussion around what we might think of as a small unit of instruction and trace our way through an instructional sequence. For convenience, we will break our instructional sequence into four stages.

1. Introduction to the topic
2. Presentation of information (topic content)
3. Learner manipulation of information
4. Review and feedback.

1. Introduction

A diagram can be used to prepare the learner for the content that will be presented in a unit of instruction by providing:

- an *advance organizer* that presents a very generalized representation of the ideas to be presented in the unit
- a *summary* of the main points that occur in the unit
- an *analogy* that helps the learners relate their existing background knowledge to the new material they will encounter
- *examples* that embody key aspects of the material to be presented in the unit.

2. Presentation of information

Once the learner has been introduced to the general topic area to be studied, diagrams can play a central role in presenting and explaining the new content by:

- *providing* information that would not normally be available to the learner, either because the learner has not encountered the subject matter before or because normal exposure to the subject matter does not reveal certain of its important features
- *simplifying* the content so that the learner is not overwhelmed by its complexity (reducing the number of pieces of information the learner is asked to deal with at one time)
- *organizing* the content into appropriate groupings so that the learner does not have to deal with a myriad of seemingly unrelated pieces and can more readily see important patterns in the information
- *isolating key aspects* of the content so that the learner's efforts are concentrated on what is most important without having to wade through a whole lot of irrelevant material
- *directing attention* to important features of these key aspects so that the learner is guided to use the presented content information effectively
- *emphasizing* particular features of the content so that they are more readily noticed by the learner
- *converting abstract* information into a more familiar and accessible *concrete* form.

In addition, diagrams can also be used for further presentation of *examples* and *analogies*, but in this case they tend to be more specific than those used in the introduction of an instructional sequence.

3. Learner manipulation of information

Effective instructional programmes involve more than simply giving the learner a single presentation of a whole lot of new information. They also require the learner to *manipulate* the presented information in some way (learner activity). This manipulation may range from simple repetition to sophisticated problem solving based on extensive transformation of the original material. Diagrams can play a role in this process by supporting mental activities such as:

- *comparing and contrasting* items of information to help learners recognize important similarities and differences (grouping and discrimination)
- *generalizing* from a variety of specific examples as part of the development of conceptual knowledge
- *linking* individual items of information together in meaningful ways
- *building coherent mental models* of the subject matter by making explicit the internal and external relations involved
- going beyond the presented material to make *inferences or predictions*
- *simplifying* things that look complex at first glance so their underlying basic principles are made clear
- providing additional *alternative representations* of material (redundant encoding)
- *consolidating learning* by means of practice and application of material dealt with in the presentation stage
- *facilitating transfer* of the presented information into other contexts
- *modelling* the types of *mental processes and learning strategies* that learners can use to help them better understand or remember the presented content.

It is worth noting here that the diagrams referred to are not confined to those provided in the instructional material itself. As will be shown later in this book, *diagrams drawn by the learner* (either partly or completely) are potentially very useful instructional resources.

4. Review and feedback

Diagrams can help learners 'look back' on the subject matter to refresh their memories and judge how effective their learning has been by providing:

- a *summary* that captures the major themes and key pieces of information dealt with in the instruction
- *questions* that allow learners (and instructors) to determine the overall effectiveness of the instruction.

In developing diagrams for an instructional sequence, the instructional designer should be able to justify each diagram in terms of the types of instructional functions (such as those given above) that it will serve. The more explicitly you can describe the instructional functions, the more likely you will be to produce diagrams that are both effective and well supported by other aspects of the instructional resource.

Analysing the content

General content analysis is an important part of any instructional design procedure. However, when designing a diagram it takes on a particular meaning. There are three key aspects of the content that need to be analysed:

1. The *entities* (or 'things') that are to be represented in the diagram
2. The *relationships* (associations or links) between those entities
3. The *qualifiers* which specify more precisely the nature of the entities or relationships.

Let's take our example of the pepper mill to see what this means.

Entities

Suppose that we are going to design a structure diagram for the pepper mill to show its component parts and how they are arranged. You might start by compiling a written list of all the bits and pieces that make up the pepper mill (or in another context, with less everyday subject matter, you may be supplied with this information from the subject expert). This is your raw list of entities that may end up in your diagram. The question to then ask yourself is 'how many of these parts can I safely remove from the list?' since one of the characteristics of a good diagram is *economy*.

However, in removing entities, you need to remember that the student should be left with enough in the diagram to be able to construct a coherent 'story' about the subject matter. This is especially important if the *structure* diagram is being presented as a preliminary to a later *process* diagram that explains how the parts of a device interact when it is operated. For example, the shaft mount on the pepper mill secures the shaft to the handle so that when the handle turns, so does the shaft and the grinder mechanism attached to it.

Another reason for not discarding some entities is that they may provide a *context* for the rest of the depiction, even if they are not important in themselves. They can help the viewer work out what it is that they are looking at, especially if the diagram deals with aspects of the subject matter that are not normally visible. These contextual entities may be drawn in a different style from the main entities that are being depicted to signal their role in the diagram. For example, if we wished to focus on the structure of just the grinding mechanism of the pepper mill, we might still include part of its surroundings to help the viewer locate the area being depicted and relate it to the rest of the pepper mill.

Relationships

A diagram depicts all relationships, no matter what their true nature, by means of graphic elements (shapes with particular *visual* properties) that are arranged in space. In other words, it uses the *visuo-spatial* characteristics of the display to represent relationships ranging from those that are indeed visuo-spatial in real life to those that have no visual or spatial character. For example, in Figure 4.1, successive pieces of the pepper mill (knob, handle etc) are shown as having been moved away from the body of the mill as it is taken apart. However, the five depictions of the pepper mill arranged diagonally on the page

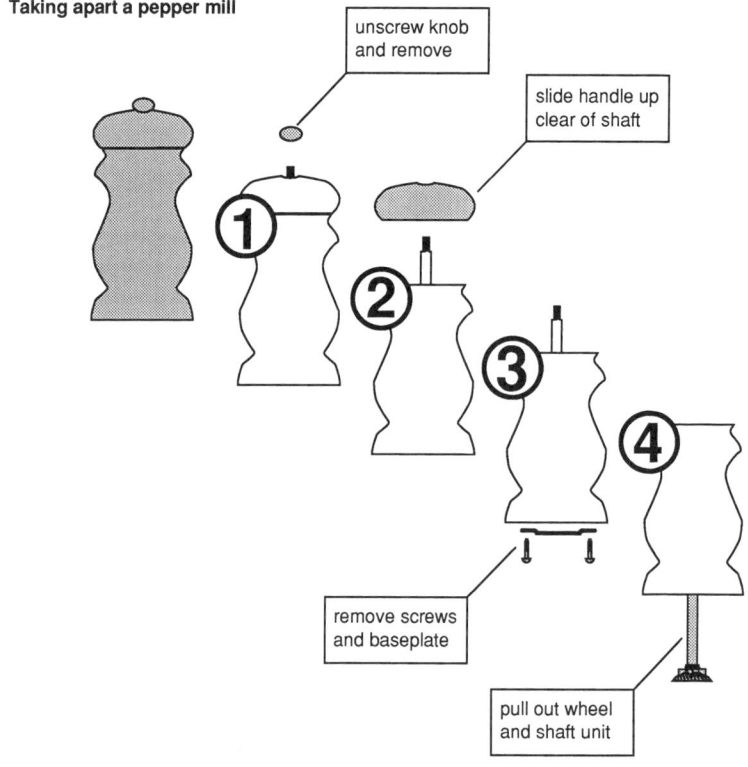

Figure 4.1 *Five different states in the dismantling of a pepper mill. These states are actually separated in **time** but this diagram replaces the temporal relationship with a spatial relationship.*

are intended to stand for a separation in *time* rather than space. Rather than being the same pepper mill placed in five different positions (or even five different pepper mills!), the arrangement indicates five successive 'snapshots' of the same pepper mill as it is progressively dismantled.

In analysing the content to be depicted in a diagram, we need to sort out both the *visual* relationships of the content that exist in real life and the *non-visual* relationships that may also be shown in a visual form. Rather than trusting to intuition in developing the diagram, it makes sense to write down the various relationships that are involved in the content. In some cases, you may simply wish to show that various items belong to each other conceptually, while others are less closely related. The use of space to represent conceptual relatedness is appropriate here. So, items that have a close relationship to each other (such as belonging to the same category of information) can be positioned near to each other. Cause–effect relationships can also be represented in diagrammatic form where the cause of a change is positioned as the left-hand part of the diagram and the effect as the right-hand part.

Qualifiers

In certain cases, it is important that the learners are given some quite specific information about the entities or relationships to be represented in a diagram. For example, it may be important that they know what the entities are made from (such as the fact that the toothed wheel and grinding compartment of the pepper mill are made out of metal) or that they have fairly precise information about the relationships between two or more entities (such as the effect of the vertical position of the toothed wheel on the size of the grinding gap).

These qualifications of entities and relationships can be included as part of the depiction to make the diagram more meaningful. For example, the use of different types of shading can signal the presence of different materials where this is an important consideration. In addition, the especially significant aspects of relationships can be heralded by various types of graphic highlighting.

Focusing the objectives

A vital part of effective diagram design is to be quite clear about what the diagram is trying to help the learner to *do*. You can't expect to develop a clear objective for the diagram at your first attempt. In fact, you may find that you begin with a fuzzy idea that needs to be focused progressively.

It helps to write down formally the objectives for each diagram in much the same way as you would if you were designing a text-based resource. Also, try defending your reasons for including the diagram to a colleague. If you find yourself falling back on reasons such as 'we've always put this sort of diagram in here' or 'the learners appreciate having plenty of pictures to break up the text' or 'there's a big gap here in the text and a diagram would help the page layout', you should probably do some serious thinking about the instructional objectives of the diagram. Sort out in very specific terms just what the diagram will show the viewer about the subject matter.

Two important questions need to be asked here. Firstly, what *class of instructional objective* is to be addressed? As with any aspect of instructional design, the author should be clear about the performance that a learner will be expected to be able to exhibit as a result of the instruction. For example, is our objective to:

(a) increase a learner's knowledge of the parts of a particular car engine,
(b) develop the learner's skills to carry out a repair on that engine, or
(c) help the learner understand the principles that underlie the operation of car engines in general?

Secondly, we should ask what *type of diagram* is best suited to dealing with the desired objective. For objectives (a), (b) and (c) given above, *structural*, *process* and *conceptual* diagrams respectively would be appropriate.

Process diagrams

In Chapter 1 we saw that structural diagrams and process diagrams were two important classes of depiction. We looked at a structure diagram of a specific pepper mill which showed its component parts and the way they were arranged. Although you probably *could* have used that diagram to help you work out the series of events that occurs when a peppercorn is ground into grains of pepper, that was not the *intention* of the diagram. Now we'll consider how a process diagram might differ.

The structure diagram ignored the dimension of *time* that is central to the depiction of a process. If we wanted a diagram that showed the process of milling pepper, we would need to find a way to represent *change* over time. For example, over the time covered by the grinding period, the peppercorn is changed from a whole state to a fragmented state. The content of a process diagram is therefore not quite the same as that of a structure diagram. Look at Figure 4.2 to see one way in which this pepper milling process might be represented in a diagram.

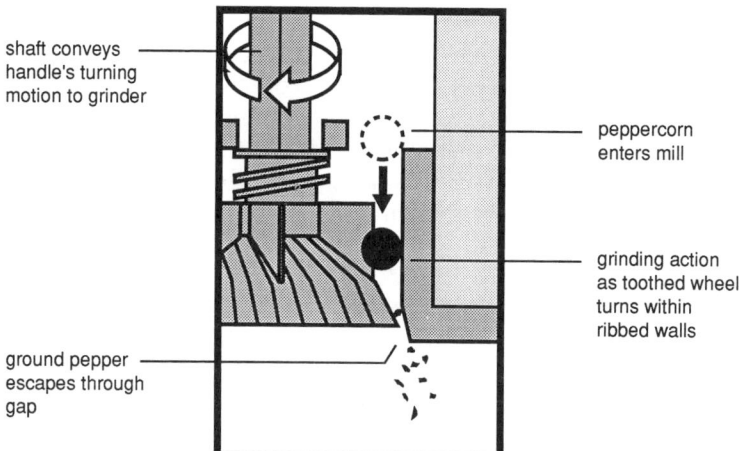

Figure 4.2 *Pepper grinding process. A process diagram concentrates on events rather than the structure of the subject matter. So, this diagram therefore assumes that the learner has previously studied the structure of a pepper mill.*

Notice the following aspects:

- the labels refer to what is *happening* rather than identifying these objects

- only those parts of the objects that are immediately relevant to the process are shown
- the same object (a peppercorn) is shown more than once
- some special symbols and graphic treatments have been introduced to help depict the process.

Although this diagram deals with the same item that was presented in the earlier structure diagram (a pepper mill), its objectives are very different. Because it is trying to do different things, it also is designed quite differently. Its depiction of the process by which the pepper is ground really assumes that, as viewers, we *already know* about the structure of the pepper mill. For example, we know the identities of the pepper mill's parts, how they are arranged and connected, what the whole pepper mill and each of its major components consist of and how many of each type of component it contains. So, the likelihood that viewers will understand this process diagram is very much determined by the *context* set by the preceding structure diagram. However, viewers must also work out the meaning of some new entities (such as the arrows and the dotted circle) which serve special explanatory functions. These entities are not to be taken literally as real objects but rather are explanatory additions that indicate dynamic aspects of the process.

Conceptual diagrams

While a structure diagram typically deals with a *particular* object or situation, a conceptual diagram deals with *abstractions or generalizations* that capture the shared essence of a whole range of conceptually related specific instances. For example, pepper mills come in a great variety of shapes and sizes. They are also made from a range of different materials ranging from wood to clear plastic. However, they are all similar in certain respects, despite this individual variation. As Figure 4.3 shows, they all have a grinding mechanism, a cavity for storing the peppercorns and a handle to turn the grinder. This diagram uses shading to identify common attributes which go together to make up the concept of a pepper grinder. The grinding mechanisms are shown in dark grey, the peppercorn storage in white

DESIGNING A DIAGRAM

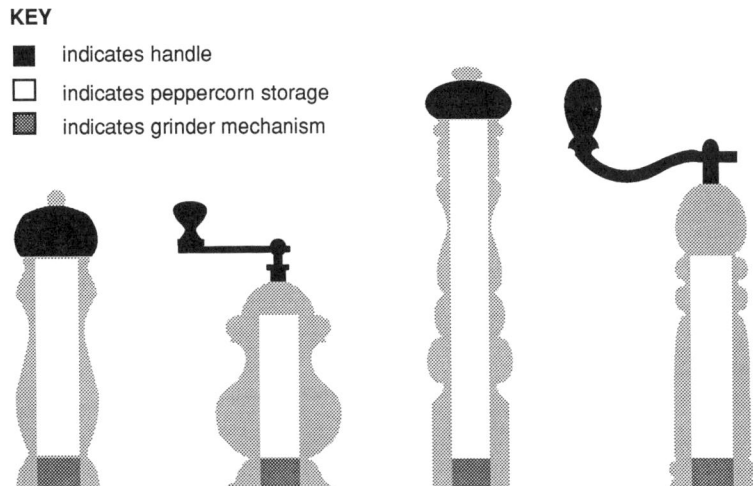

Figure 4.3 *A concept diagram showing the essential similarity of structure that exists across a range of differently shaped pepper mills. Note how the use of a key aviods the need for messy labelling.*

and the handles in black. The light grey indicates the different shapes and sizes of the pepper mills.

Increasing explanatory power

Diagrams use a range of *graphic transformations* that make them better able to explain the subject matter. These sometimes deliberately alter the 'normal' characteristics of the subject matter so much that it is unrecognizable. For example, try to work out what is depicted in the diagram that is shown in Figure 4.4. Here the diagram so extensively alters the subject matter that special training is required in order to interpret it correctly. In fact, it is a type of diagram that is used in the field of choreology to notate the dancer's movements that make up a ballet's choreography. Figure 4.5 shows you this

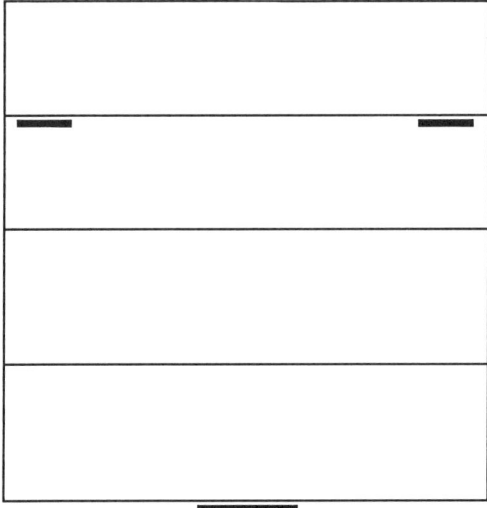

Figure 4.4 *What is represented in this diagram?*

choreological diagram in a form that is more accessible to non-choreologists.

The transformations that are involved in increasing a diagram's explanatory power are not all as extreme as in the previous example. However, as we shall see later, even 'mild' transformations can be a source of difficulty to those who are unskilled in dealing with them. A 'correct' interpretation of a diagram involves the viewer taking proper account of the transformations rather than taking them as a literal representation of the subject matter.

Let's look at some of the main types of transformations that can be used in diagrams to help them explain the subject matter more effectively. We have already seen from the discussion and example diagrams presented so far that each transformation involves some form of alteration of the normal appearance of the subject matter. Most transformations can be thought of as performing one of the following general types of explanatory functions:

1. *Simplifying* the subject matter by the omission of irrelevant information and by the organization, regularization and stylization of relevant information
2. *Amplifying* the subject matter by the addition of information that is not normally available and by the use of special symbols that aid interpretation
3. *Tagging* particular aspects of information by giving special meanings to graphic components that make critical aspects of entities, relations and qualifiers explicit and more noticeable.

Below is a list of some specific transformations that you can use to increase the explanatory power of diagrams (you should recognize a few of these from earlier parts of this book).

- Leave out as much as you can in the way of entities, relations and qualifiers (but remember to include enough contextual information so that viewers will know what they are looking at). Instead of trying to cram everything into a single complex diagram, consider using a series of simpler diagrams, each of which deals with a different aspect of the subject matter.
- Simplify each of the components you are left with after throwing away the irrelevant material.
- Make components more regular in their shape, size and orientation than they would be in real life so that irregularities with no explanatory significance are removed.
- Use details selectively so that the level of detail shown will act to signal the importance of information. The viewer's attention tends to be drawn to more detailed sections of a diagram.
- Vary the line weight and drawing style to provide visual cues about the relative importance of different types of information. Contextual information can be drawn with a thinner line or lighter tone than information that is more central to the explanation.
- Rotate the subject matter as a whole to provide views that reveal additional information.
- Distort parts of the subject matter by bending or twisting to help show information that would not normally be accessible in a particular view.

SUCCESSFUL INSTRUCTIONAL DIAGRAMS

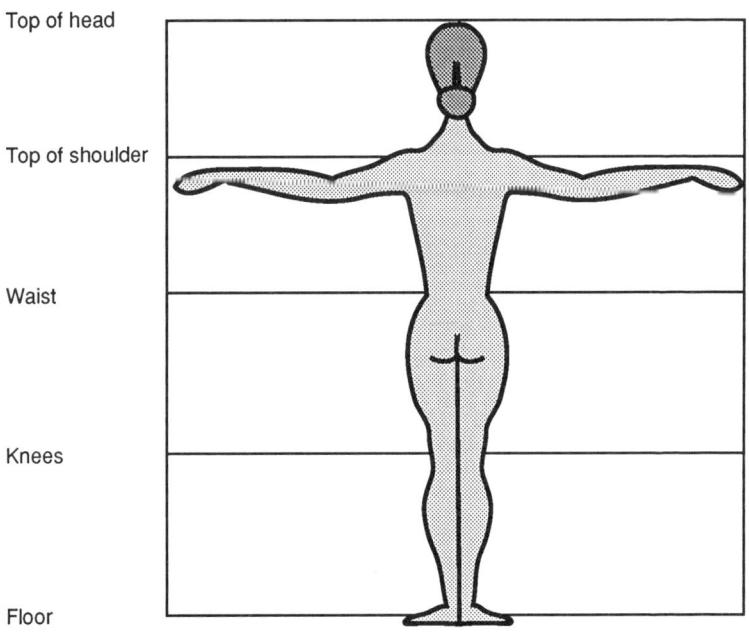

Figure 4.5 *An alternative representation of the subject matter shown in Figure 4.4 that most people find more accessible.*

- Make sections of the subject matter transparent to let the viewer see the relationship between surface and underlying structure.
- Show cross-sections or cut-away views that give additional information on normally hidden aspects of the subject matter.
- Use an exploded view that separates all the entities and lays them out so that their relative positions, sequence and orientations can be observed.
- Show the progressive dismantling or assembly of the subject matter.
- Introduce graphic entities that give a visible form to entities which are normally invisible in the real world.
- Add other graphic material such as arrows, boxes and shading to direct the viewer's attention or reading direction,

show important groupings of information and distinguish key parts of the subject matter.
- Alter the scale of components of the subject matter so that aspects of particular significance are readily visible or can fit in with the overall treatment used for other aspects of the diagram.
- Magnify important regions to focus attention, reduce the amount of information the viewer has to deal with at one time and make critical features readily visible.
- Distort aspects of the subject matter that need to be emphasized so that they are more readily attended to by the viewer.
- Exaggerate features that have a key role in the diagram's explanation of the subject matter.
- Use a mixture of views of a single component of the subject matter.
- Superimpose entities that are normally separate to reveal subtle differences that exist and which may otherwise be difficult to detect.
- Use multiple images of the same entity within the diagram to show different states which the entity goes through in a process.
- Combine different stages of a process into a single depiction.

Effective instructional diagrams typically use a mixture of several of these techniques. However, they need to be used with discretion so that a diagram does not become just a confusing and bizarre array of graphic tricks. The above list is certainly not exhaustive; there are many other techniques that have been used to help diagrams present their subject matter more clearly so keep your eyes open and build up a file of useful ideas.

5 Producing a Diagram

Producing initial ideas

When should an author or instructional designer start to think about the diagrams that will form part of an instructional resource? Too often, most of the detailed thinking about diagrams is left until quite late in the development process. Some instructional designers make only general decisions about diagrams while they are preparing a manuscript (such as where diagrams might be fitted and what their overall content would be). A result of this approach is that material to be presented via diagrams is not treated as central to the exposition but rather as 'icing on the cake'.

If diagrams are to realize their potential as tools for instruction, they need to be seen not as optional extras, but as *integral* components of an instructional resource. Their contribution to the total instructional resource needs to be considered carefully from the outset and should drive the way they are developed and used. The systematic design of instruction generally involves a thorough analysis of the audience, content and objectives at an early stage of the design process. This analysis process should extend to the diagrams used in a resource so that the distribution of responsibility for explanation between diagrams, text and other instructional components produces the best effect for the instructional task at hand.

Brainstorming the subject matter will help you identify the sorts of things that need to be covered in diagrams. Once you have generated an unstructured collection of ideas, look for some way to organize this material by finding parts of the subject matter that belong together and may form the basis for individual diagrams. For example you may work out that you are going to need structural, process and conceptual diagrams to deal adequately with a topic such as pepper mills.

Once you have clarified the subject matter and purpose of each diagram, you need to start considering the graphic material that will make up the diagram. This is clearly necessary if you are to carry out all stages of the diagram's development yourself. However, even if you plan to have a skilled graphic artist develop the finished artwork, you need to provide her or him with some quite specific reference material upon which the diagram can be based. Don't assume that artists can draw anything you may request of them without suitable references just because they are artists. It is also usually not a good idea to leave artists to hunt around themselves for suitable material. The chances are that they will not have a sufficient understanding of the subject matter or purpose of the diagram to do this successfully. If the subject matter for a diagram is a physical object (such as a pepper mill), you may be able to begin with a set of photographs that show the object in different ways. For example, the object could be shown:

- from a variety of views (side, top, bottom, profile, three-quarter etc)
- with different levels of detail (long shot and in close-up)
- assembled, partly disassembled and as separate parts (with each of the parts shown in close-up and from a variety of views)
- under different lighting conditions (to highlight or clarify different aspects)
- in various states (if it is a working object that undergoes visible changes as it carries out a task).

The different states may be internal (between different parts of the same object) or external (between the object and its environment). Taking a video may also help if a process diagram is to be developed. Particular frames can then be chosen which best capture key stages of the process to be depicted.

Photographs such as these are a resource for diagram development. You can combine aspects from them in different ways and so give the artist a composite depiction that gets as close as you can to the material you want included in the diagram.

Developing the entities

The raw material in the photographs should act as a reference but remember that the strength of a diagram over a photograph is that it can reveal aspects of the subject matter which are impossible to show photographically. This is what you are after in order for the diagram to be instructionally more powerful than a series of photographs. The depiction in the photograph should have been heavily transformed by the time it becomes part of a diagram (as per the types of transformations listed at the end of Chapter 4).

For many diagrams, producing an initial sketch to set out the main features you want to depict is relatively straightforward. However, with others, you may feel that coming up with your initial ideas in the form of a sketch is beyond your artistic abilities. In these cases, you can build up a composite depiction from your photographic references. It is a good idea to use photocopies of the photographs rather than the originals since there may be many modifications and a lot of experimentation required. Relevant portions of the photographs can be enlarged (or reduced) during photocopying then cut and pasted to form the required composite. Sections of these copies can also be used as the basis for simplification of the subject matter by using a suitable pen to draw over key features of the photocopy to highlight them or distort them in ways that provide appropriate diagrammatic emphasis. Similarly, non-essentials can be blotted out and annotations made directly on the photocopy to further guide the artist. It will probably take several cycles of this process until you are satisfied with the result. You may wish to trace the material so as to produce an uncluttered version that is more like a line drawing. Because the amount of modification made in this sort of process can make details of the subject matter almost unrecognizable, it is wise to provide the artist with plain copies of the original photographs appropriately keyed to the modified composite.

PRODUCING A DIAGRAM

Using photographs as the source of initial ideas is not possible in some cases because some of the subject matter is simply not available to be photographed. For example, it may be too small (like electrons), too far away in space or time (like the surface of the sun or the geological separation of the Earth's land masses in the process of continental drift), intrinsically invisible (like sound waves travelling through the air) or an abstract concept that is a product of someone's mind (like democracy). In cases like these, the visualization of the subject matter may rely upon a verbal or mathematical description as its starting point. As a result, the author has little alternative but to do the best they can in the form of a sketch with appropriate notes attached.

An important step in designing a diagrammatic representation of subject matter for which direct images cannot be obtained is to build up as much information as possible about its components and structure. This needs to be accompanied by assigning visuo-spatial representations to the subject matter. In some instances, there are existing images which can be used as a starting point (such as the existing physical features and locations of the continents as the result of continental drift). In others, purely geometric shapes can be used as arbitrary tokens to stand for particular entities whose actual shapes are unknown. Between the extremes of incorporating actual shapes and using ones that are largely arbitrary, a visualization that has some accepted association with the subject matter can be used (such as using pictograms for people and buildings in a diagram intended to represent the concept of democracy).

Care needs to be taken in deciding which entities you will include in a particular diagram and which you will leave out. Although your goal is to produce an economical depiction that has been stripped down to its bare essentials, you need to keep in mind how difficult a diagram might be for the learner to interpret. For most diagrams, depiction of some of the context of the components of interest is necessary. So an important early step in the design process is to decide on how much 'inessential material' you need to show in order for the viewer to pick up the context. We need to help the viewer to be able to think to himself or herself such things as 'so the thing that I am looking at is . . ., and I'm looking at it from . . ., and the particular section shown here is situated . . .'.

For example, when you show a close-up that consists of only part of the subject matter, you need to give the viewer some way of relating that whole to the part shown in the magnification (see Figure 5.1). This connection between part and whole should be made so that the relation is as simple and direct as possible.

Simplification in diagrams can be a problem for the viewer if taken too far or applied purely mechanically. Elements of the subject matter that are in reality distinct can be mistaken for one another because they become too similar when greatly simplified for the purpose of a diagram. In this case, care needs to be taken to retain (or introduce) some distinctive feature that will permit them to be easily distinguished. This is especially important in diagrams that simplify the content down to an arrangement of basic geometric shapes (such as lines, boxes or circles).

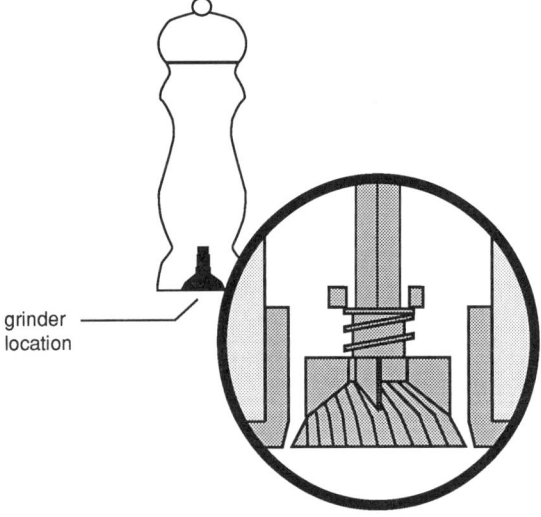

Magnified view of grinder
Peppercorns drop into grinder from storage area of mill.

Figure 5.1 *Learners need to be able to locate the region being shown in close-up so they can understand the magnification in terms of the part–whole relationship involved.*

A special class of entities that are particularly valuable in diagrams are not derived directly from the subject matter. The role of these entities is to help the viewer interpret the information provided in the diagram. They include:

- boxes and circles
- arrows
- dashed or dotted lines
- labels and explanatory notes.

Boxes and circles are used to group a set of entities, draw attention to specific features and signal the presence of transformations such as magnification.

Arrows are used for a wide variety of purposes ranging from specifying the sequence the viewer should use in 'reading' the diagram or bringing to attention features that should be noticed, to representing various aspects of change such as physical movement or cause–effect relationships). An arrow's placement, pointing direction and physical characteristics are all important in determining its significance within the diagram. Because the arrow is a widely used diagrammatic symbol with a vast number of different meanings, you should take special care to avoid confusing the viewer when using arrows in your diagrams. For example, it is usually better to use plain lines rather than arrows to indicate the part of a diagram being referred to by a label. If you really need to use an arrow (where it is the only practical way to identify a very specific region), make sure that the attached label says something like 'arrow shows . . .'. Ensure that arrows within the same diagram that have different meanings are given quite different graphic treatments and that the individual meaning of each type is made quite explicit to the viewer.

Dashed or dotted lines are used as reference lines to help the viewer make comparisons by making explicit the differences in the size, shape, position or orientation of entities.

Labels and explanatory notes are used to identify entities, add extra information at the place where it is needed, or guide the viewer's interpretation. Included in this category are numbers, letters and symbols that are used for purposes such as making cross-references between particular parts of the diagram and the main body of the accompanying text.

Treatment of entities

The type of graphic treatment that is given to the entities in a diagram can help the learner read the diagram and develop a meaning consistent with that intended by the author. We have already touched on the degree of realism used to depict the entities. In some cases the diagram entities are given a similar appearance to the subject matter they represent (such as where the purpose of the subject matter is to aid identification of an object or to help distinguish between different regions on an object). For example, a diagram that shows you how to assemble a new household appliance should have a degree of realism that is sufficient to help you to choose the correct component at each stage of the assembly process and find where each of the components should go when you are fitting them together. If the diagram is so simplified and lacking in visual clues about appearance that you can't identify the different parts shown in the diagram or tell one end of the appliance from the other, correct assembly will be difficult. This example demonstrates the importance of considering carefully the context in which the diagram is to be used and the need for thorough field testing of the diagram's effectiveness in the situation in which it is actually used.

In other cases, more arbitrary graphic forms (including geometric shapes) are used to represent the subject matter, particularly where the *relationships* between the entities are of primary importance (such as in a flow diagram that shows the stages in a process). Many diagrams of this type use entities that are meant to act simply as tokens rather than trying to give much idea of the actual appearance of the subject matter represented. So, in a diagram intended to represent the concept of a two-party democracy, a circle symbol might be used to represent each person who votes for one party while a square is used to represent each person who votes for the other party. In this example, it is the numerical relationship between the different symbols that is important. However, the use of more abstract or arbitrary symbols does rely on the learner being able to interpret those symbols appropriately. For this reason, you need to consider carefully the background of your target learners before using this type of graphic vocabulary.

The use of arbitrary geometric shapes or forms that are very abstracted rather than 'more informative' graphic entities also has the potential to help the learner focus on the *overall* arrangement rather than on its details. This is a version of 'seeing the wood for the trees'. Where the aim of instruction is to give the learner a *broad overview* of the subject matter, such as its general organization, the inclusion of detailed depictions of specific items may distract attention from the higher-level considerations. For example, Figure 5.2 is intended to show three important *general* features of pepper mills, not to deal with details of the construction of any particular mill. This high-level purpose would not be well served by a more detailed diagram.

As well as deciding on the *type* of entity you will use to represent a particular component of the subject matter, you should also think about how it will be *rendered*. What sorts of lines and shading do you want used in drawing the entity?

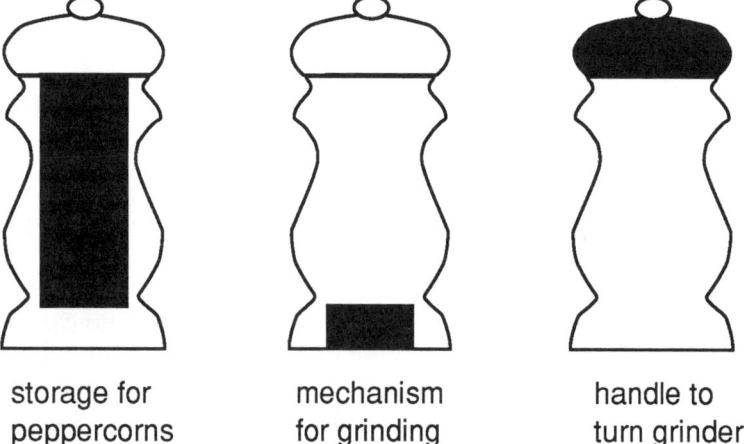

| storage for peppercorns | mechanism for grinding | handle to turn grinder |

Figure 5.2 *A high-level overview of the main sections that make up a pepper mill. This type of diagram can prepare learners for more detailed depictions that follow.*

Overall, diagrams are generally distinguished by an easily recognizable diagrammatic style (as we saw in Chapter 1). They typically are drawn in a manner that gives a precise appearance by using neat lines, regular shapes, a degree of stylization and a rather formal use of shading. Within a particular diagram there is usually a range of ways in which line and shading (and possibly colour) can be used. This variation should provide clear *signals* to the viewer about how different parts of the diagram are meant to be interpreted.

In general, solid lines should be used for more important parts of the depiction and to help viewers clearly distinguish one entity from another. So it is usually a good idea to draw the *external* surfaces or boundary of an entity more boldly than its internal parts. If an entity is not central to the main 'argument' of the diagram but has been included to provide *context*, this needs to be signalled to the viewer by the way it is rendered. It is important that this material is 'knocked back' in some way so that it does not compete with the main subject matter for the viewer's attention. Techniques for rendering this secondary contextual material include:

- drawing it in an outline representation using a lighter line weight than used for the main subject matter
- using dotted lines for the outline
- using a screened outline so that the contextual material is not printed as a solid line (but rather as a shade of grey, for example)
- using a lightly shaded *area* in the background that gives the overall shape of the contextual material.

It is often useful to shade the main content of the diagram (as opposed to the contextual material) to indicate various relationships that exist between entities. For example, entities that are related because they belong to the same group or class can all be shaded with the same level of grey or with the same colour to indicate their association (even if they are spatially separated in the diagram). In applying renderings to entities, beware of techniques (such as some forms of cross-hatching) that add visual confusion to the diagram by making areas seem very 'busy'. Unfortunately, various computer graphics packages include a number of these fancy patterns in their range of rendering treatments and novices seem strangely compelled to use them, despite the disastrous visual effects. Treatments that use uniform shading are preferable since they help to keep the display simple. For example, up to five conceptually distinct areas in a diagram could be identified by using three different shades of grey plus black and white.

Resist the urge to use a huge range of different rendering techniques in a single diagram. This adds to the visual complexity and makes the diagram difficult to process. If you are tempted to do this, you may need to ask yourself why you are trying to include so much information in the one diagram. Perhaps the subject matter needs to be split across a series of simpler diagrams. Take another look at your subject matter and see if it can be broken down into a number of broad conceptual groups. Each of these may be the basis for its own diagram.

The supplementary entities in a diagram (such as arrows, boxes and circles) that are added to help it explain the subject matter more effectively need to be clearly distinguished from the main entities that are features of the subject matter itself. For example, if you draw a ring around a key feature of a display to attract the learner's attention to it, you need to make it obvious that the ring is not itself part of the subject matter. It is often a good idea to make these supplementary entities stand out by using quite heavy line weights or distinctive shading (a contrasting shade of grey or colour). Keep in mind that your intention should be to send out an unambiguous signal to the viewer about the purpose of this entity within the overall scheme of things in the diagram.

Another aspect of a diagram that you may like to consider as an 'entity' is the empty space (or background). Although you may not think this important for its own sake, it can play a part in the overall readability of the diagram. At a very fundamental level, you need to make sure that there is sufficient *contrast* between the background and the entities presenting the subject matter of the diagram (this may be especially critical where colour is being used extensively in a diagram). You should also be sure that there is sufficient distinction between 'field and ground'. This means that the viewer must easily see what is meant to be the subject matter of interest (the field) and what is just the background (or ground). So be careful that the amount of detail and graphic emphasis in the background is kept to a minimum. The amount of empty space between entities should also clearly signal which entities are meant to 'go together' (close spacing) and which are meant to be treated as separate items (wide spacing).

Assembling entities into a diagram

One of the potential strengths of diagrams is that they can help to make instruction more effective by taking advantage of our well-developed capacity to process *visual patterns*. However, to take best advantage of our pattern-processing capacity, the entities comprising the diagram must be arranged in patterns that facilitate appropriate processing by the learner. A poorly arranged set of entities can make it difficult for the learner to find his or her way through the diagram, or may produce an inappropriate interpretation of the subject matter. An arrangement that is neat and orderly in a general sense helps make it easier to read any diagrammatic display. However, this general level of organization is not the only aspect to consider in devising a suitable arrangement of the entities. The arrangement must also set the entities out in a way that highlights important features that are specific to the subject matter of a particular diagram and helps direct the learner's processing of that content.

A number of different (and sometimes competing) things need to be considered in assembling the entities into the spatial arrangement they will have in the diagram. These include the following.

- The real-life spatial arrangement of the material to be represented in the diagram.
- The non-spatial relationships present in the material that are to be represented spatially in the diagram.
- The spatial aspects of the transformations that will be used in the diagram to present the content more powerfully.

- The clarity that will result. Will each of the entities and spatial relationships be easily distinguished or will a cluttered arrangement be produced?
- The information load that the arrangement will place on the viewer – remembering that we start to have difficulty in processing information effectively if we are given much more than about seven information chunks to deal with at one time.
- The way target learners will be likely to read the diagram. This will be in line with the learners' expectations about where critical pieces of information are likely to be located and the sequence in which the information will need to be explored.
- The overall graphic design that will result from the particular arrangement. Will it form an aesthetically balanced display that uses graphic conventions in an effective manner?

Some of these considerations need to be dealt with on a case-by-case basis (such as the real-life arrangement of the depicted material) and others have already been dealt with earlier in this book. However, there are a number that we will look at here in more detail.

Non-spatial relations

The arrangement of entities in a diagram is often changed from their real-life arrangements to show non-spatial relationships in a spatial manner. In general, this approach makes two assumptions:

1. the *ordering* of the entities represents some organizational principle present in the real-life non-spatial relation (adjacent entities being more directly related than separated entities); and
2. the *distance* between entities represents the closeness of the relation (smaller distances indicating closer relations).

Two widely used formal types of arrangement in diagrams are *sequences* (where the material is arranged along a single line) and *networks* (where the material is in a two-dimensional arrangement). Common examples of sequences include timelines, diagrams that show the stages in a process and those that arrange the subject matter in order of a particular concept such as size or complexity). Networks are typically used where multiple relations are to be represented. Common examples include tree diagrams, classification schemes and diagrams that show an organizational hierarchy.

However, there is a whole range of much less formal arrangements used in diagrams which still make use of the ordering and distance effects. The important thing in using such arrangements is to make them readily accessible. Be consistent in the way you use space to represent non-spatial relations and help learners process the diagram appropriately by actually telling them what the arrangement shows. There are four common types of non-spatial relations that are depicted spatially in diagrams, as explained below.

Temporal: Differences in *time* are shown as differences in *position*. A sequence of events is most commonly depicted by a left (earlier) to right (later) arrangement, although a top to bottom arrangement is sometimes used. Where possible, keep these temporal diagram sequences consistent with the conventional types of overall reading patterns people are used to for text (left to right, top to bottom). Avoid the temptation to create fancy sequences that wander 'interestingly' across the page simply for graphic effect. Where a sequence cannot easily be fitted to either of these simple arrangements, the order of its steps should be clearly indicated by devices such as numbers or arrows. This is especially important where more complex cyclic arrangements (such as in life-cycle diagrams) are used. As well as showing the *order* of the events, diagrams can show the relative time interval between different events (temporal *closeness*) by using different distances.

Hierarchical: Items can be arranged according to their significance in a situation or process. A diagram of the social structure and power relationships that existed in Ancient Egypt from the Pharaoh down to the slaves would exemplify this hierarchical type of arrangement.

Part–whole: One way to represent the organization of some instructional content is to show the way the whole can be broken down into its component parts. For example, instead of showing the pepper mill in an assembled form as a structure diagram, we could have firstly divided it into its three main sections (turning mechanism, peppercorn storage and grinding mechanism) then further divided the turning and grinding mechanisms into their individual components, as shown in Figure 5.3. The advantage of this diagram in emphasizing the functional relationship of the parts to the whole must be balanced against the effect it has in disrupting the real-life spatial relations that were depicted in the structure diagram shown in Chapter 1. For this reason, this form of taxonomic diagram is often used along with other diagrams that depict the physical arrangement of the parts.

Class membership: Diagrammatic classification schemes can be used to categorize the subject matter as a convenient summary

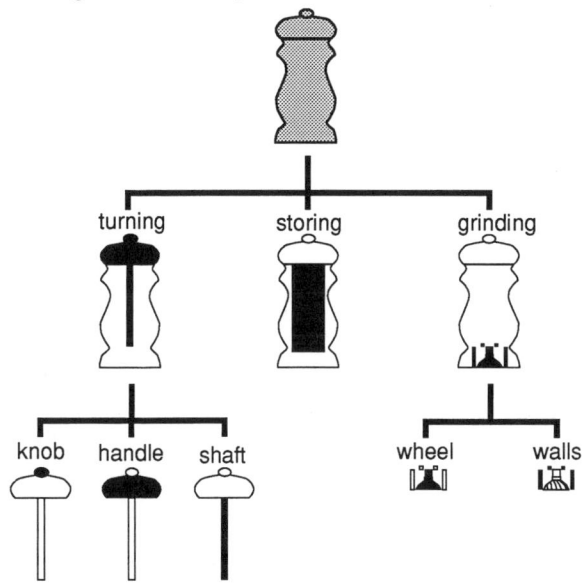

Figure 5.3 *This part–whole diagram shows relations involving the main sets of functional components of the pepper mill. It makes use of multiple representations of the mill and its various parts.*

of broad similarities and differences. Although these diagrams may look much the same as part–whole diagrams (having the same tree structure), they deal with a collection of different, whole entities rather than breaking down a single entity into its component parts. For example, in Figure 5.4 all the items can be used in the kitchen for subdividing food into smaller pieces. However, they work on different principles and so can be classified into different groups. We are not interested here in the parts that make up each of these devices, simply in the similarities and differences in their principle of operation. Each item is shown as an icon that functions as a token (a label would have done equally well). The importance of the spatial arrangement of this diagram lies in the way conceptually related items are organized into groups.

The arrangements discussed above present the subject matter in a way that exposes significant relations which are key features that need to be appreciated in developing an understanding of the content. However, the diagram designer can also use spatial arrangements that are intended to invite the viewer to process the material in the diagram in certain ways

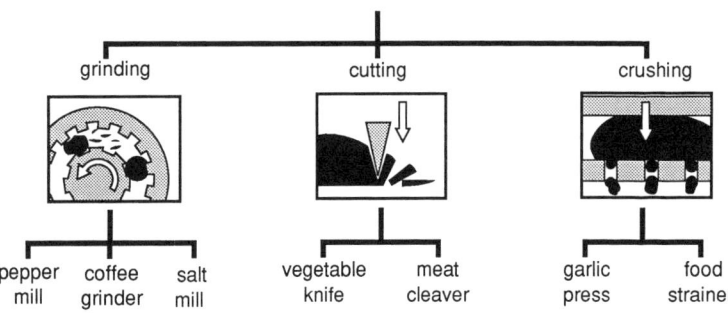

Figure 5.4 *This classification diagram arranges the subject matter into classes according to conceptual similarities. Note use of both icons and labels to specify content.*

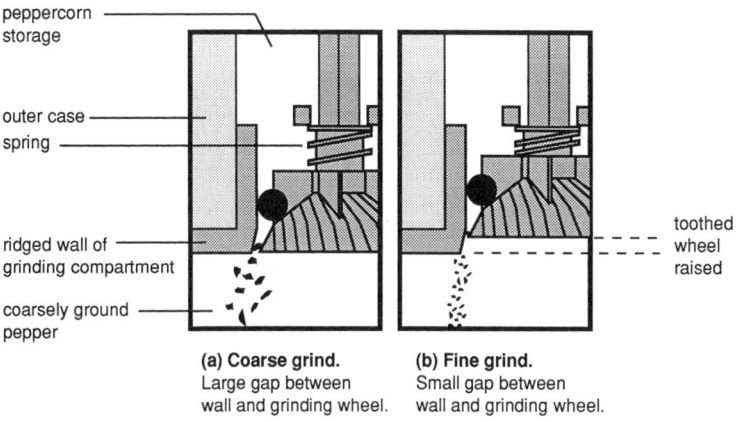

Figure 5.5 *A side-by-side arrangement of very similar material 'suggests' they be compared ('spot the difference'). Note the use of exaggeration and dotted line cues to help the viewer.*

that will help promote effective learning of the subject matter. For example, Figure 5.5 shows how a side-by-side arrangement can be used as an invitation to the learner to compare and contrast two representations, especially if most of the elements in each half of the diagram stay the same

Technological aids for diagram production

A range of ways of capturing, processing and developing images exists that greatly simplifies the job of developing diagrams. We have already seen that photographs can be used to provide an artist with references for diagram development. They can also be used to help authors develop their own diagrams if used in conjunction with some of the graphics programs available for computers. The first task in using computers to develop diagrams from photographic images is to get the image into the computer. Here are some ways in which this can be done.

- Tape an overhead transparency made from the photograph on to the screen of the computer so that it can be used as a template guide for copying parts of the image on to the screen with a mouse or similar input device.
- Trace over a photograph attached to a graphics tablet connected to the computer.
- Use a scanner to produce a digital copy of a photograph so that it is in a form which the computer can store (and manipulate). Flat-bed scanners can also be used to make copies of real objects, provided they are small enough and not too deep (in this case a white cloth draped over the object can be used in place of the scanner lid).
- Use a digital camera to take a digital image that can be entered directly into the computer.
- Connect a video camera to the computer via an appropriate video board and use a frame grabber to capture a still image of an object that is to be used as the basis for the diagram. This will give you a digital copy of the image that you can store on computer disk and later process in a variety of ways.
- Make a video of the object that is to be shown in the diagram (shooting from different angles and distances) then use a frame-grabbing board to capture still images from the video tape.

Once the photographic image is 'inside' the computer (in digital form), it can be manipulated in a number of ways with suitable software. The initial goal is to produce line drawings of relevant parts from the photographs that will be used as a basis for constructing the diagram. A variety of software programs allow operations to be performed on the image such as:

- altering the brightness and contrast to make the image more clearly defined (for example, reducing the image to a simple

black and white version that emphasizes the overall shape for easier tracing)
- sharpening the image
- finding the edges of the image and automatically outlining them
- converting the image to a form suitable for tracing (either manually or using an auto-trace program)
- electronic editing of a number of images to produce a composite (similar to the procedure described above for photocopies except that it is done via a computer).

For final preparation of the artwork, it is an advantage to use a flexible graphics program that allows you to perform extensive manipulations of individual diagram components. You need to be able to scale portions of the image, distort them, copy them in various ways, group (and ungroup) them and easily set up accurate alignments. In addition, you need to have ready control over individual line thicknesses, shading types and lettering.

In general, programs that define images by means of mathematical descriptions rather than as a collection of pixels are preferable for producing high-quality diagrams. This means using graphics packages described as 'drawing' programs rather than those described as 'painting' programs. Particularly useful are programs which allow lines to be drawn as bezier curves which provide great flexibility in constructing diagrams and give crisp images when printed on higher-resolution printers.

6 Instructional Diagrams in Context

Visual characteristics of different media

Our discussion so far has implicitly assumed the use of *conventional print media* for presenting instructional diagrams. While the general principles we have discussed are applicable to a range of instructional media, some media have special characteristics that can either enhance or restrict the possibilities for diagram design. For example, a book can show much finer detail in a diagram than can be shown on a video screen. However, a book relies on a static presentation of the subject matter whereas a diagram on video can be animated.

In developing diagrams for media with technical features that impose constraints on the presentation of material, the designer needs to be aware of these constraints and work around them. Conversely, when diagrams are to be designed for media that offer new opportunities for display, these opportunities should not be ignored. A diagram that would be effective in a book should not simply be transferred as it stands to another medium. Generally some form of modification will be necessary to ensure that the change of medium does not result in either decreased instructional effectiveness or a failure to take advantage of the special possibilities of an alternative medium. Some of these modifications arise from fundamental technical considerations (as in the book versus video example mentioned above) while others are a result of the way different media typically are used by both presenters of information and viewers.

Media constraints in diagram design

Different media have different physical and perceptual characteristics which define what we can do with diagrams within each medium. This is not a case of one medium being uniformly 'better' than another as a means of presenting instructional diagrams. Rather, we can think of each medium having a distinctive profile of strengths and weaknesses that need to be taken into account when working within that medium.

However, what is *possible* and what is *instructionally effective* are not necessarily the same. In what we may call 'dynamic' media (such as video and computers which make possible the presentation of moving images), there can be a temptation to use animated diagrams just because the technology makes it possible to do so. Arguments for using animation in this way may reflect a rather narrow concern with the motivational ('attention grabbing') aspects of this type of presentation to the exclusion of wider educational considerations. For example, it may be that a series of static diagrams in a book that presents key stages in a process is instructionally just as effective as an animated version shown on video (and perhaps considerably less expensive to produce and more readily accessible to the viewer who doesn't happen to have a video player handy). Further, the quality of instructional design that is embodied in a diagram (animated or otherwise) is central to its potential instructional effectiveness, irrespective of the medium. So, a poorly designed diagram that lacks effectiveness in a static form will not necessarily be improved simply by turning it into an animated presentation. There may well be fundamental design problems that limit its usefulness as an aid to instruction.

The following list gives some of the more common characteristics that need to be taken into account when designing diagrams for different media.

1. *Resolution* In practical terms, this refers to the fineness of the image that can be satisfactorily presented in a medium. A medium that can show very fine detail is said to have a high resolution. One way to describe resolution is in terms of the number of dots per inch (dpi) that can be displayed. Print materials typically have medium to high resolution (laser

printers produce a resolution of 300 dpi or better while the speciality printers used for very fine printing produce resolutions of thousands of dots per inch). In contrast, the resolution of most computer screens is much lower (for example, 72 dpi). If a detailed diagram with finely drawn lines was transferred from a book to a computer screen without modification, it is likely that some detail would be lost. Even worse resolution problems can occur with video, with the additional difficulty that the image 'breaks up' into a juddering display if closely spaced lines are used.

Another aspect of resolution that has to be considered is the way resolution worsens quite dramatically with distance. So a number of individual lines drawn close together on an overhead projector transparency which are perfectly clear to those in the front row of an auditorium may merge into a broad band for those at the rear.

2. *Colour* Although colour printing and the use of colour in other types of media are becoming much less expensive, there are still many applications in which the expense of colour is not justified. Much can be done with black, white and three or four well-contrasted shades of grey to give a range of possibilities for coding different types of information on diagrams; colour is by no means necessary in many cases (although it may be preferred for its motivational and aesthetic effect).

Even when colour is available, there may be restrictions on the way it can safely be used within a particular medium (as is the case with video images in which certain colours and colour combinations produce undesirable effects). If there are no technical problems in displaying colours in a particular medium, human factors and instructional effects need to be carefully considered. For example, certain colour combinations (such as bright primary colours) can cause visual fatigue or interfere with the ease of reading a display (as occurs when there is insufficient contrast between background and foreground). Further, the use of colours in a purely decorative manner may not be compatible with their more fundamental instructional function in signalling important or related units of information to the viewer. Certain colour combinations (red with green, for instance) should be avoided because of the problems they would cause for the small percentage of viewers who are colour blind.

3. *Orientation and proportions* The proportions and fixed orientation of a display medium such as video limit the possibilities for presenting a diagram. In a book such as the one you are now reading, a tall diagram can be printed down the page ('portrait' orientation) while a wide diagram can be printed at right angles to the normal page layout ('landscape' orientation). The reader has simply to rotate the book to an appropriate angle. However, the fixed screen of a video with its set proportions (four units wide by three units high) does not offer this possibility. So, compromises must be found when attempting to present diagrams whose proportions or orientations do not conveniently fit on a video display screen.

4. *Movement* Diagrams that incorporate movement can be particularly useful for depicting a process (typically, a series of related events that leads to some outcome). So, an animated diagram of a peppercorn being progressively torn into pieces between the toothed surface of a pepper mill's grinding wheel and the ribbed wall of the grinding compartment would be an effective way to show the continuous nature of this process. All stages of the process could be shown explicitly with the peppercorn gradually working its way lower in the grinding compartment as its size decreases. Showing some aspects of the process via a *static* presentation would require a series of diagrams with an accompanying explanation and could demand considerable mental gymnastics on the part of the viewer during interpretation. Unfortunately, animated diagrams can be much more difficult and expensive to produce than static diagrams. In addition, important events or significant states in a process may actually be more difficult to discern if simply shown as part of a continuous animation.

5. *Closeness of view (part versus whole)* A secondary effect of the limited resolution of media such as computers is that the learner is unable to zoom in and out smoothly in a manner which

duplicates what is possible with printed materials. To take a closer look at a complex or detailed diagram in a book, the page can be moved closer to the viewer in a process that is both intuitive and barely perceptible. However, a similar diagram cannot be treated the same way when displayed on a computer. If the whole diagram is shown, its finer details disappear because of the resolution limits of the screen. In order to take a closer look at some of these details, computer programs typically provide some type of 'magnifying tool' ('zoom in, zoom out') that can be used to enlarge a chosen part of the image. This can lead to a very fragmented experience for the viewer which contrasts with the smooth way in which a high resolution printed diagram can be explored at different levels of detail. Part of the difficulty of coping with such computer presentation of diagrams is that the viewer cannot rely on natural peripheral vision to assist the exploration process.

6. *Presentation durations (learner control)* When presentations are made via media such as linear video (videotape) and overhead projectors, it is the presenter or presentation device largely setting the pace. A diagram presented in this way typically is shown for a relatively brief period of time with the learner having little control over how long the diagram is visible. In contrast, a book allows the learner to decide how long s/he wishes to study the diagram and so provides more flexibility in the way the diagram can be used as a learning tool.

7. *Exploration freedom (learner control)* A related limitation with videotape and overhead projectors is that learners have little control over the order in which they can explore diagrams and the supporting materials associated with those diagrams. Nor do they have much choice as to how often each of these resources can be referred to in the study process. This lack of learner control places a great responsibility on the designer to develop diagrams which are readily accessible under these conditions. However, it is far more difficult for a book to guide learners through a diagram than it is for a video which can make use of techniques such as panning and zooming to direct attention in potentially productive ways.

Working around media constraints

Just as it is important to know about the constraints that exist in different media, diagram designers also need to consider carefully how best to work around these constraints so that they can still produce instructionally effective diagrams. To give a comprehensive treatment of how these constraints can be handled across the whole range of instructional media is beyond the scope of this book. So rather than attempting to deal with all media, we will concentrate on video presentation as an illustrative example.

The following recommendations should be considered when designing or modifying a diagram for presentation via video.

- Make each diagram as simple as possible, preferably showing a single main idea only. See if a complex diagram can be broken down and treated as a number of simpler diagrams.
- Where complex diagrams cannot be avoided, build them up gradually.
- Use a series of diagrams showing the same subject matter at different levels of detail.
- Minimize the use of labels; make the labels short, and use large, bold, well-spaced lettering (preferably sans serif) for the text. A suitable voice-over may be used to reduce reliance on text.
- Make the diagrams as large as possible, preferably filling most of the screen (but see the next recommendation).
- Keep the diagram well away from the border of the screen to avoid losing material from around its edges.
- Plan the diagram so that it fits the proportions of a video screen (four units wide by three units high).
- Use large bold shapes and heavy lines.
- Clearly define each separate component (perhaps by using a bold outline or a sharp colour contrast).
- Ensure that adjacent lines are well separated from each other and avoid finely textured patterns (such as cross-hatching).
- Incorporate in the design provision for video techniques such as panning and zooming to work around the limited resolution and fixed screen shape.

- Use a related range of subdued colours to distinguish different parts of the diagram rather than a highly varied mixture of bright colours. Keep background colours fairly neutral and well contrasted with foreground colours. Where bright colours are needed to highlight particularly salient information, use 'video-safe' colours to avoid problems such as 'bleeding across' (merging between) different colours. (These colours are less saturated than normal, typically only 75 per cent of normal saturation.)
- Be careful that the diagram is shown for an appropriate time (not so long that boredom sets in and not so short that the learner does not have time to process its information).

Other common forms of presentation (such as overhead projectors and computers) have their own particular constraints and various ways have been found to work around them so as to produce effective instructional diagrams. You may find it useful to build up a list similar to the one given above for other presentation media.

Computer-based diagrams

Although some of the newer media of instruction have disadvantages such as limited resolution and a fixed orientation with respect to the viewer, they do allow us to provide experiences in which learners can *interact* with the diagrammatic material presented. This interaction allows the learner to 'do' something to a diagram and have the diagram respond in some way. For example, a static diagram presented on a computer screen may be designed to contain areas that act as 'hot spots' which are sensitive to touch or some other form of signal such as a mouse click or a key press. When the learner touches such a region of the diagram, the computer responds with an appropriate action. This might be anything from a simple response, such as revealing a label that identifies the touched part, to a complex series of actions such as animation of the whole diagram to illustrate a process. Such responses can not only act to motivate the learner and keep him or her engaged with the material, they can also have other instructional benefits concerned with their explanatory effectiveness.

Other forms of interactivity for the learner that can be built into instructional diagrams presented by computer-controlled technologies include:

- moving selected items in the display so they can be positioned on another part of the screen
- changing the orientation of a displayed item (rotating, inverting)
- increasing or decreasing the size of a displayed item
- adding or deleting items on display (added items can be either selected from a list provided or drawn by the learner)
- coding items of the display with particular types of identification (such as a distinctive type of shading)
- 'pulling' or 'pushing' on a particular region of a display in order to cause a reaction.

For instruction to be effective, learners should be actively involved with the learning materials rather than passive recipients of delivered content. The interactivity that can be provided by computers has been heralded as of great importance to instruction, particularly where the learner is in a self-study situation. So, the provision in diagrams of interactive features which will involve the learner has the potential to make diagrams more effective as tools for learning.

The mere provision of large amounts of interaction does not in itself promote effective learning. The instructional effectiveness of these interactions is primarily due to their *quality* rather than their quantity. For example, suppose a diagram of a pepper mill on a computer screen is designed to reveal an appropriate descriptive label each time a part of the pepper mill display is clicked on with a mouse. Compared with a fully labelled diagram in a book, this style of presentation undoubtedly reduces the load of information that the learner must deal with at one time and so probably has some fairly primitive instructional benefits. However, this long series of mouse clicks presents little challenge for the learner in terms of the quality of *thinking* required to make each response. Rather, it is not much more than a succession of mechanical actions that probably involves only very low level decision-making and little *mental* interaction with the content.

In contrast, consider a task in which the learner is presented on the computer screen with a set of 'parts' that are to be used to build a diagram of a pepper mill. By using the mouse, each of these separate diagram parts can be moved around the screen during assembly of the whole diagram. The mental processes required in order to produce an appropriate series of interactions in this task would be much less trivial than those used in the previous example. Deeper forms of processing such as would be required in this construction activity are associated with superior learning. In developing interactive diagrams, designers need to go beyond their physical structure to consider the nature of the interactions that a learner will have with the diagram and the depth of mental processing such interactions are likely to elicit.

Animated instructional diagrams

In previous chapters, we have assumed that diagrams are essentially static displays. However, many of the types of subject matter that typically are represented in diagrams have a dynamic aspect, such as the events involved in a process, or can be made clearer by some form of animation, such as the assembly of a structure or the development of a concept.

In this section we will not deal with animations that are designed simply to engage the learner's attention and sustain motivation by the use of spectacular graphic effects. This is not to suggest that these effects do not have their place in an instructional resource. Too often, however, animated sequences serve little other purpose. This is a huge waste of the potential of movement and change in graphic images as tools for explanation and the development of understanding. The function of animated diagrams in an instructional resource needs to be much more than visual titillation if that resource is to use diagrammatic presentation effectively.

As we saw earlier in this chapter, just because animation is possible, it doesn't necessarily follow that we should use it on every possible occasion. So how do you choose when to use a static diagram and when to use an animated diagram? Here are some suggestions.

When to use a static diagram

- When no dynamic aspect is involved (such as when structure only is required and the structure is relatively simple).
- When the subject matter is dynamic but where you want the learner to explore it in more detail than is possible in a dynamic display. This allows the learner to move his or her attention to different parts of the display to deal more effectively with aspects of the subject matter that are (a) complex, (b) unfamiliar or (c) familiar but not properly analysed by people in most circumstances.

When to use an animated diagram

- When dynamic subject matter is involved (having previously established knowledge of the components and structure of the subject matter).
- When the subject matter is static but needs further explanation of aspects of its components and structure that are not always obvious to the untutored observer.

Suppose you are designing diagrams for a dynamic medium such as video or computer and have a general idea that using animation can somehow make the diagrams instructionally more effective. If you are accustomed to thinking about diagrams as static resources, how might you begin to make use of movement and change as additional ways to help a diagram be even more powerful instructionally? You may find it useful to think of animation as yet another transformation that you can make in the subject matter to make its important aspects clearer to the learner (an extension of the way transformations are used to increase the explanatory power of static diagrams). In other words, having used a variety of transformations to produce a static diagram that acts as a visual summary of the subject matter, what specific additional *dynamic transformations* can you introduce to heighten the presentation's effectiveness?

A key function that animations can serve in instructional diagrams is to help the learner *explore the subject matter more fully than would otherwise be possible*. When people try to find out about a subject, they can explore it in different ways. Think about how someone might approach finding out more about a pepper mill. They may start in a relatively detached manner by just having a good look at it. By looking at it more closely and systematically than they would normally, they may notice aspects of which they were previously unaware. Later, they may explore it more interactively by manipulating it in various ways (turning the handle, altering the fineness of grind adjustment, taking it apart, manipulating its internal components etc). Well-designed animated diagrams can be used to mimic some of these approaches.

Uses of animation

Let us have a look at some specific situations in which animation could be used to explore the subject matter more effectively.

- For seamless changing between different views of the subject matter. This not only allows more of the subject matter to be explored, it can also make it easier for the learner to understand the relationship between these different views so that a coherent whole can be built up in the mind from the different parts (separate views). For example, a close-up of the base of a pepper mill showing the grinder can be smoothly linked to an overall view that gives its context by tipping the mill backwards from a side view so that its base swings towards the viewer.

- For exposing normally unavailable material to reveal additional key information. Here, the transformation involves more than a simple change of viewing angle. Rather more drastic 'operations' are carried out, such as dismantling an object, taking a slice through it to reveal a cross-section or causing its outer layers to become transparent. (Each of these could be very useful in our pepper mill example.) As well as establishing the context of the transformation in a relatively painless way, this type of animation can also demonstrate the transformation *process* itself (instead of merely showing the *results* of that transformation). In this way, the learner can see how an often quite strange diagrammatic representation is linked to the world of everyday experience.

- For highlighting key information in the diagram by some form of dynamic change. This approach is designed to focus the learner's attention on critical aspects of the subject matter that may otherwise go unnoticed. Our attention is naturally attracted to change such as movement. Techniques include changing the colour of key entities to make them stand out (including flashing them briefly, providing it is not overdone), having an entity shake or pop forward out of its usual position to 'present itself' to the viewer, or drawing a ring around part of the diagram to identify a feature that is being described.

- For building up or breaking down the subject matter in order to help the learner deal with it more effectively. Because our capacity to deal with information is limited, learners are likely to be overwhelmed if presented with a complex diagram that deals with unfamiliar material. Simple animation techniques can be used to build up a diagram in stages so that too much information is not presented at one time. For example, we might start with an outline diagram of a pepper mill and bring in components a few at a time (preferably so that they form meaningful 'chunks' of related material). The reverse of this approach can be used when we are dealing with familiar material that we wish the learner to look at in new ways. In this case, the whole diagram would be presented and then animation techniques used to break it up in a manner that highlighted the aspects we wished to focus upon in the analysis.

- For leading the learner through a diagram in a way that is most likely to result in an appropriate interpretation of the subject matter. For example, in presenting an overview of the main sections of a pepper mill, an animation could start with the handle section being turned then move the view down along the rotating shaft until the grinder was reached. The view could then zoom in on the grinder mechanism to see how the rotation of the toothed wheel caused the peppercorns to be ground.

- For demonstrating a sequence of events. Here the natural series of changes that occur in the subject matter is reflected but, to make the animation instructionally effective, various distortions may be used. Two important types of changes that can be depicted are changes in *form* (such as a peppercorn becoming smaller as it is ground) and changes in *position or orientation* (such as the toothed grinding wheel rotating as the pepper mill's handle is turned). Distortions that can be used to help the explanation include:
  1. leaving out unimportant parts of the sequence
  2. changing the speed of some events so they can be seen more clearly, and
  3. breaking the whole sequence into key sub-sequences.

- For allowing the learner to interact with the subject matter. This can let the learner find out about the subject matter by seeing how it responds to various types of exploratory manipulation. For example, in a computer simulation, the learner might be able to click on the handle of the pepper mill to see what happens when it turns, or drag the toothed wheel upwards to see how this affects the fineness of grind. This technique can also be used to evaluate learning by having the learner carry out tasks that require correct manipulation of the diagram (such as moving a set of randomly placed entities into the correct arrangement). This type of animation is generally restricted to computer-based forms of presentation that can both detect a learner action and perform the processes needed to respond appropriately.

7 Integrating Diagrams in Instruction

Diagrams in an instructional system

Diagrams typically form only part of a wider instructional system and, in order to contribute effectively to that system, they need to be well integrated with its other components. These other components might include such things as:

- printed text
- a spoken commentary or sounds
- photographic images (still or moving)
- real objects or situations
- a live instructor
- other learners
- various devices that permit learner input (such as a mouse or touch screen on a computer).

The diagram and its accompanying resources may also be destined for use in quite different instructional situations. Compare these two examples:

1. A diagram presented in a video that forms part of an open learning package intended for individual learners to use without an instructor.
2. A diagram on a worksheet designed for use in a classroom situation with an instructor who both discusses the diagram with the students and closely supervises the way they work with it.

In the first example, the diagram (and its accompanying video material) needs to 'stand alone' far more than the diagram in the second example. With a live instructor present, a diagram can be introduced and explained in a way that is appropriate to the existing knowledge and skills of the particular group of learners concerned. In addition, the learners' diagram interpretation can be monitored so that help and feedback may be given when problems in understanding are detected. In a situation in which a capable and sensitive instructor is available, little other support for the diagram may be required.

However, when this type of flexible and contextually specific support is not available (as would be the case with the video example), the instructional designer is faced with the challenge of providing a suitable substitute. This role must be filled by material that 'surrounds' a diagram (in this case, the material that precedes, accompanies and follows the presentation of the diagram).

As we saw in Chapter 1, diagrams are not like more everyday pictures. For a novice in a particular subject area, diagrams typically require considerably more effort than do other pictures in order to 'read' them successfully. However, additional effort alone will not make a diagram yield up its secrets if the learner does not direct that effort appropriately. Because diagrams can only go so far in 'explaining themselves', it is important to provide effective learner support. Although the video example we have chosen here is a rather extreme example of a stand-alone instructional resource, some level of learner support is needed even for materials such as textbooks that are used as an adjunct to traditional classroom teaching. For example, consider the situation in which the learners have been set a section of a textbook to study by themselves out of class time. In most cases, their only help in processing any diagrams they encounter will be provided by the text that accompanies those diagrams.

Irrespective of the presentation medium, when a diagram is expected to stand on its own, the learner will generally need to be:

- *prepared* for the diagram (What is the learner going to be shown and why?)
- *guided* through its interpretation (What does the learner need to do in order to build up an appropriate meaning from the diagram?)

- helped to *integrate* the information in the diagram with the rest of the subject matter (What does this diagram contribute to the learner's overall understanding of the instructional topic?)

These three functions should always be considered, whether the instructional resource is something as traditional as a textbook or something as up-to-the-minute as a computer-controlled interactive multimedia experience. They are essentially the functions that any competent instructor would expect to perform when introducing a new diagram to a group of learners. In other words, as far as the learners are concerned, diagrams are *not* assumed to be 'transparent' learning resources whose meanings are obvious (even though these meanings may seem perfectly obvious to the instructor). Rather, diagrams are seen as resources that are *potentially* valuable to learners *provided they can use them properly*. Fulfilling a diagram's potential requires the learner to pay careful attention to the material in the diagram and to use a systematic, thoughtful and informed approach to its exploration. These requirements in turn depend on the learner being given some form of appropriate guidance.

Integrating text and diagrams

In Chapter 1, we identified our overall aims in using diagrams as: to help learners develop appropriate understandings of the subject matter and to assist them in its recall. Because a combination of text and diagrams is commonly used in instructional resources, we need to be clear about the way they are meant to act together to present the subject matter and help learners to process it in instructionally effective ways.

Two important functions that diagrams can have when used with text are to:

- *parallel the text* so that they can reinforce the material presented in the form of text, compensate for a learner's lack of text reading skills or provide an appropriate mode of presentation for learners who prefer visual representation.

- *provide additional information* to that provided in the text because of their greater suitability as a means of representing particular aspects of the subject matter (such as spatial characteristics and certain types of non-spatial relationships).

In this section we will concentrate on the second of these two functions since it poses more potential problems in terms of integrating text and diagram. Here, the text and diagram are complementary sources of information. The learner's task involves getting the best out of each source and combining these two sources mentally into a coherent single set of information. This combination can be thought of as the building of appropriate links between the two types of information. A minimum prerequisite for this linking process to be carried out successfully is that the author has made it relatively easy for the learner mentally to process together these sources. The associated diagram and text ideally should be:

- as close as possible physically, and
- connected by explicit references between the text and the diagram.

In the case of resources such as books, having the diagram and text as close as possible means preferably on the same or facing pages, or on a separate sheet (possibly a foldout) that can be referred to irrespective of the text page being read. Using numbers, letters or symbols on the diagram and corresponding markings in the text can reduce the need to cover the diagram with labels when you need to provide detailed explanations. However, it does produce a greater physical separation between the text and diagram.

For other media such as video and computers, it may be difficult to provide enough space on the display screen for both a clear diagram and all of the text associated with the diagram. One possible solution is to use a series of small sections of text placed next to the diagram, with each new section of text replacing the previous one while the diagram remains on the screen. Different parts of the diagram can be highlighted or arrowed as they are referred to in the series of text blocks, to help the learner link the two forms of representation. Another technique is to use a voice-over instead of text. While this has the potential of allowing the learner to concentrate on the diagram more fully, care needs to be taken that the voice-over does not overload the viewer with information. With computer presentation, interactive techniques can be used that produce explanatory text for a diagram 'on demand'. For example, 'pop-up' text can be incorporated that appears only when the learner identifies a particular part of the diagram (a 'hot spot' that is activated by a mouse click or finger contact on a touch screen). With this approach, provision can also be made for the learner to choose a level of explanation that is appropriate to her or his current needs.

Complementing diagrams with text

Just as diagrams can be regarded as a complement to text because they contribute additional information, so text can be seen as a complement to diagrams. In the interests of clarity and simplicity, text that is essentially part of a diagram (such as labels and captions) is typically brief. More detailed matters are dealt with in the body of the text. However, in some uses, the distinction between these different types of text disappears, as in the use of extended labels which go further than simple identification of parts of the diagram. In this approach, the 'labels' become substantial blocks of text (often boxed) that provide a detailed description or explanation of particular regions of a diagram. Used skilfully, this approach has the virtue of keeping the textual material closely linked to the part of the diagram to which it refers, making it easier for the two to be integrated. However, there is no natural sequence in which successive text blocks need be read (as there would be if they formed paragraphs in a text body). Consequently, if sequence is an important part of the exposition, clear guidance should be given to the order in which these text blocks should be read (by using numbers, arrows etc).

Text can serve a variety of functions as a diagram adjunct including the following.

- Identifying the entities represented by the various graphic components of the diagram; for example, the names of the different parts of the pepper mill.
- Describing aspects of the depicted material that are either difficult to represent pictorially or better represented by text. These include relationships or qualifiers that have no obvious visual manifestation; for example, the fact that the shaft connecting the pepper mill's handle and its grinding mechanism causes the grinder to rotate when the handle is turned.
- Linking the diagram to the subject matter it represents or to some other representation; for example, stating that the diagram of the pepper mill is a cross-section.
- Posing questions to the learner about the diagram; for example, asking the learner to work out how the top adjustment knob alters the fineness of grind produced by the pepper mill.
- Providing guidelines as to how the material comprising the diagram should be 'read' (or explored) and interpreted; for example, instructing the learner to follow the shaft of the pepper mill from the handle downwards to note that it is connected to the toothed grinding wheel.

Because of the importance of this last role of text in the instructional success of diagrams, it will be discussed in more detail in the following section.

Using text to guide diagram processing

One reason why explicit references between text and diagram are advisable is because, even when highly motivated to learn, some people use less than ideal approaches to deal with explanatory information. This is amply illustrated by the well-known saying: 'If all else fails, read the instructions'. It's natural to try to get by with the minimum of bother if at all possible (after all, that's being efficient isn't it?). So it can be with a combination of text and diagrams; learners may not use them in a way that is entirely systematic or thorough. We should never assume that all learners will see our diagrams as an integral part of the presentation of the subject matter or that they will know how the diagrams need to be processed for best effect. If the diagrams and text have been carefully designed to complement each other, learners who take short-cuts such as largely ignoring the diagrams (or treating them in a superficial manner) will inevitably miss out on important aspects of the subject matter. Similarly, relying largely on the diagrams to the exclusion of the text would also be unsatisfactory. Explicit cross-references between the text and diagrams can help ensure that the learner's efforts are directed to both types of resources. As well as encouraging this comprehensive approach to the instructional materials, cross-references can also indicate the following.

- What *sort of a representation* we are looking at. For example, we might say, 'This is a highly simplified version of the inside of a pepper mill that shows a side view of its three main sections', or, 'Now let's turn the mill upside down to see a more detailed diagram that concentrates on the grinder, this time seen from below'. This form of commentary can be useful in helping to prevent the learner becoming lost as we move from one view or representation to another.
- What *parts* of the diagram are most useful to look at; for example, 'Notice the knob at the top of the pepper mill. Its role is to adjust the grinding mechanism'. In animated diagrams, it is often a good idea to guide the learner to focus on important aspects of the events which are taking place; for example, 'Watch what happens to the fineness of the pepper coming out of the bottom of the mill as we vary the adjustment knob at the top'.
- In which *order* the various regions of the diagram should be explored; for example, 'Look at the left-hand part of the diagram first so you have an overall idea of the pepper mill's general structure, then move to the box on the right that gives a bottom view showing details of the grinder mechanism'.
- How to *relate* the different parts of the diagram to each other and to the diagram as a whole so that the information can be assembled mentally into a coherent overall meaning; for

example, 'Compare the size of the pepper grains shown in the left-hand side of the diagram with those shown on the right', or, 'You can see that despite the variation in the external appearance of the different pepper mills, they all have the same basic structure'.
- How to *think about* the diagram in the most productive manner; for example, 'Don't become bogged down in the detail of this pepper mill diagram. It's easiest to think about the diagram in three sections; the middle section where the peppercorns are stored, the bottom section where they are ground into pepper and the top section that lets you turn the grinder'.
- How learners can *monitor their progress* in dealing with the material being presented in the diagram; for example, 'Check that you can match all the parts shown in this diagram with pieces of the pepper mill you have just taken apart', or, 'You should now be able to remove the grinder from the base of the pepper mill; if it is still not free, refer to the diagram to see if you have removed all the necessary screws'.

Integrating diagrams with other resources

Although text will probably remain the most common resource accompanying diagrams, many situations require that the diagram be integrated with non-text resources. These can range from other forms of visual representation, such as photographs, to the actual object that is depicted in a diagram. Our pepper mill diagrams can provide us with a rather light-hearted example of such a situation. Imagine that you are to have a dinner party tonight but find that your pepper mill is not working properly. Fortunately you remember that the book you've just started reading on instructional diagrams contains some diagrams about the structure and operation of a pepper mill that looks a bit like yours. Desperate to avoid social embarrassment, you thumb through the book, find a likely looking diagram and start work on repairing your pepper mill.

Now let's think our way through this example. For the diagram to be successful in helping you work out how to repair your pepper mill, you need to be able to put together in your mind the diagram and the real object. We'll confine our attention to the structure diagram shown in Chapter 1 (Figure 1.4). This diagram should help you to find the various parts of your pepper mill (What do they look like and where will you expect to find them?) and give you a better idea of its construction. Ideally, it should be easy for you to map back and forth between the features of the diagram and those of the real object.

In various more formal learning contexts, a similar integration between diagrams and real objects, states, events or processes is required as part of the instructional strategy. Consider a person learning to assemble, disassemble or modify (repair) a device from a self-instructional module that incorporates a series of explanatory diagrams. Not only should the learner be able to recognize and locate each of the individual components shown in the diagram, s/he also needs to understand how they are related in various ways. For example, s/he will have to know how to orient parts correctly (involving the use of a spatial relation) so that they can be fitted together or taken apart. So, the diagram must give sufficient clear guidance in how the real-life parts need to be manipulated.

Of course, the idea of helping learners to carry out this integration process is not confined to interrelating diagrams and reality. A similar process would be necessary to integrate a diagram with a different *representation* such as a photograph or a graph. In one sense, interrelating a photograph and a diagram has the potential to be easier than interrelating the diagram with reality. The photograph has already been reduced to two dimensions so there are fewer degrees of freedom to worry about. However, if the photograph shows a view of the subject matter that is very different from that shown in the diagram, it may in fact be more difficult to interrelate the two representations. So our goal should be to make it as easy as possible for the learner to move seamlessly between the diagram and other representations. This allows the learner to concentrate on developing an understanding of the subject matter itself rather than on trying to work out how it is being represented.

What can we do in general to help the learner to interrelate a diagram and one or more other representations of the same subject matter? Essentially, our task is to make it easy for the learner to *compare* the representations and to *guide* that comparison in productive directions. This involves the following.

- Keeping the diagram and the other representation(s) close together in space and time.
- Making the connections between different representations quite explicit. For example, identify corresponding features by highlighting both of them and linking them graphically or symbolically (such as by drawing lines between them or by identifying them with the same symbol).
- Showing or describing things from the same view or in the same order for both types of representation. This minimizes the amount of mental manipulation the learner must do before s/he can interrelate the different representations. (People can find mental rotations and transformations difficult, which produces unnecessary interference with the process of interpretation.)
- Superimposing one representation of the subject matter on another (such as a diagram on a photograph). When presenting in a medium such as video, the diagrammatic version can be faded in on top of the photographic version which is then faded out.
- Making the transition between a diagram and some other form of representation sufficiently gradual. If the diagram is too different from the other representation, learners may have difficulty in establishing relations between the two. For example, if a highly abstract diagram is to be related to a very realistic depiction such as video footage of the real-life situation, it may be useful to provide an intermediate representation that bridges the gap between these two extremes. This approach can be particularly useful for learners who are reluctant to engage with diagrams. Here, a more realistic representation is used as 'bait' to involve the learner who is then gently moved to progressively more abstract representations of the subject matter.

A note of caution is needed here. It is very easy in one's enthusiasm to destroy a diagram's essential simplicity by 'working it over' too much. Avoid producing a jungle of interconnections, additional markings and cross-references aimed at making it easier for the learner to interrelate different representations. Keep in mind that 'simple and elegant is best'.

8 Improving Instructional Diagrams

Approaches to evaluation

It is not reasonable to expect even a very well-designed diagram to be universally effective. The evaluation of an instructional diagram needs to take into account:

- the nature of the learners who will be using the diagram (for example, are they beginners in the subject area or advanced students?)
- the medium by which the diagram will be presented to the learners (for example, will it be part of a book or included in a computer-based package?)
- the situation under which the diagram is to be used (for example, is it to form part of an open learning package or is it for use in a traditional classroom situation?).

Ultimately, the only completely valid test of a diagram's effectiveness is how well it works in a specific instructional context. However, in developing diagrams or materials that include diagrams, it is important to carry out evaluation during the development process as a basis for revision. Most diagrams will need to go through a number of drafts. This formative evaluation should involve in the development process those who play a key role, that is:

- content expert
- artist
- media consultant (such as the video director or book editor)
- instructional designer.

In addition, it is of course essential to involve the target learners. This involvement will be discussed later in this chapter.

In the discussion that follows, we will assume that you are filling the role of the instructional designer and that separate people fill the other roles. (Of course, in some situations, two or more of these roles may be filled by a single individual.)

The content expert must ultimately be convinced that each diagram gives a sufficiently comprehensive treatment of the subject matter and is free from errors. However, keep in mind that the content expert may not be in the best position to judge other aspects of the diagram. In particular, s/he may not appreciate some of your efforts to make the subject matter clearer to a learner who is a novice in the area. Remember that to the expert in a field, the meanings of introductory diagrams are virtually transparent and it can be difficult for him or her to see what you are making all the fuss about. Considerable tact may be needed here. You may even need to try some of the 'transparent' diagrams out on a few novices to convince the expert that they might be challenging. (It can be a good idea to video this rather than have the content expert on hand at the time.) When you think that all your negotiations for the development of a diagram are complete, it is still vitally important that the content expert sees the 'final' version before it goes to publication. This is because in the process of refining a diagram, the artist, instructional designer or media consultant may inadvertently introduce content inaccuracies. It is sometimes virtually impossible for a person who is unfamiliar with the content to detect such inaccuracies (which can sometimes turn the whole diagram into nonsense).

The artist will be able to advise you on how to improve the graphic design of your diagram as it goes through its drafts. Be aware that the artist's concern with *graphic* design may not always coincide with what you are trying to do with the diagram's *instructional* design. For example, the artist will probably be more focused on the aesthetic balance of the artwork across the page than on a special spatial arrangement you might have set up to depict some important explanatory relation in the diagram. However, using the artist's professional eye to tidy up your rough drafts is an important part of the revision process, so some negotiation may be needed. Be sure to keep the artist well informed about the instructional purpose of the diagram and how you are trying to achieve this. Remember that it is all too easy for the artist to make minor alterations in the artwork which can have serious instructional consequences. These alterations are not usually a result of carelessness or an attempt by the artist to impose his or her will on the diagram; rather, they come about because the artist's expertise is in the field of graphics, not in the subject matter or the field of instruction. Make sure you check artwork carefully when it is returned and be tactful about how you deal with any necessary alterations.

The media consultant can help you to make your diagrams more suitable for the constraints of the medium in which they will be presented. Wherever possible, try each diagram out in the medium for which it is destined. For example, if the diagrams are to be part of a video, see how they look on that type of display screen (don't just rely on a paper copy or an image on a computer screen). Becoming aware of the limitations of the display medium early in the development process will prevent a lot of wasted time.

In your role as instructional designer, you can use the guidelines given throughout this book to help your evaluation of a diagram design as it is developing. Draw up your own checklist for the particular medium in which the diagram is to be presented and use this as a way to begin the refining process. Early diagram drafts should also be shown to your colleagues. This will help you find the most glaring inadequacies in the drafts, some of which you may overlook because of your own biases or your over-familiarity with the subject matter.

Learner-based evaluation

Once some of the more fundamental revision of a diagram has been done, potential users of the diagram will need to be included in the evaluation. This is a critical part of the evaluation process and one where you will have to make trade-offs in terms of time and other resources. A typical approach to learner-based evaluation of instructional materials is to employ a three-stage process, as follows.

1. One-to-one evaluation in which a detailed evaluation is carried out with individual learners (but not in the context of use of the materials).
2. Small group evaluation where a limited sample representing the main types of learners likely to use the materials is employed (also completed out of context).
3. A field trial in which the material is evaluated in the actual context of use.

However, this approach is intended to be applied to instructional resources as a whole, rather than to their individual components such as diagrams. So, a finer grained approach is warranted if our intention is to improve diagrams rather than make broader-level improvements. There are a number of levels at which you can collect information for evaluating the way learners respond to diagrams:

- diagram alone
- diagram in conjunction with its accompanying instructional material
- diagram in the context of its use.

Learner-based evaluation needs to address a variety of questions. Some of these questions are quite general, such as:

- does the learner consider the diagram to be helpful?
- does the learner process the diagram sufficiently deeply overall?
- does the learner understand and remember the material presented?
- can the learner apply the material presented?

Others are more specific, such as:

- are there particular aspects of the diagram that learners find distracting, annoying or confusing?
- does the learner explore the information provided in the diagram in a productive fashion?

- does the learner deal effectively with the various transformations that have been used in the diagram?
- can the learner identify all the entities shown in the diagram and assign them an appropriate role in the diagram's explanation of the subject matter?
- can the learner locate all the important relations that exist among the diagram's entities?
- does the learner integrate material in the diagram effectively with its accompanying materials?
- can the learner translate the relations which the diagram depicts in visuo-spatial terms into their intended real-life meanings?
- can the learner go beyond the diagram and use it to deal successfully with the actual subject matter of the diagram?

We can classify both the general and specific questions given above as fitting into the following categories of evaluation.

1. The *opinions* learners have of a diagram (their reactions).
2. The *way* learners work with a diagram (their processing).
3. The direct *instructional results* of the diagram on the learners (their grasp of the subject matter).
4. The learners' *performance* based on the instructional results (the new capacities they can demonstrate).

Although these are listed as separate categories, they are not necessarily independent. For example, a learner who finds a diagram off-putting because it contains too much information may process that diagram in an ineffective manner and so develop a poor grasp of the subject matter and be unable to carry out satisfactorily tasks based on the diagram. However, other cases are possible such as where learners do well in formal pencil and paper tests of the subject matter presented in a diagram but are unable to apply what they have learned (something not of course confined to diagrams).

Ideally, learner-based formative evaluation should cover the four categories listed above. However, practical considerations usually force the instructional designer to make a choice, at least in the first instance. For example, if a diagram is to be used to teach people how to perform a psychomotor task (such as taking a pepper grinder apart), you may opt to evaluate its success directly by seeing how well the learners are able to carry out that task in practice. (Naturally you would not use this approach if the task is one that involves hazards such as danger to the learner or the possibility of expensive damage to equipment.) If everything seems to work without much trouble, you probably need to go no further. However, if learners' performance is faulty or incomplete in some way and the reason is not apparent, you should consider the other classes of evaluation.

Learners' opinions

Collecting information about how learners react to a diagram can be relatively uncomplicated. However, some simple safeguards are necessary.

- Make sure you take the time to convince the learner that it is the *diagram* that is being evaluated, not the learner (since it is usual for people to interpret a test situation that involves instructional materials as an assessment of their own performance, rather than as an evaluation of the effectiveness of those materials).
- Provide a relaxed atmosphere for one-to-one or small group evaluations so that the learners are encouraged to speak freely about the diagrams. It helps to distance yourself from 'ownership' of the diagrams so that the learners do not hold back because they perceive that any criticism of the diagram might be interpreted personally.

Although it is pleasing if learners react positively, this doesn't necessarily mean that the diagram will be instructionally effective. In fact, some consider a positive reaction to instructional materials as rather unhelpful since it gives no basis for improvement of instructional effectiveness. So, it makes sense to provide the learner with a framework that stimulates critical thinking about key aspects of the diagram's design. Approaches for collecting learners' opinions about a diagram include the use of:

- pencil and paper instruments (such as rating scales, questionnaires and open-ended responses)

- interviews using probes which target specific aspects of the learner's response to the diagram
- observations of the way the learner reacts to the diagram when using it to perform some task – it is useful to have the learner 'think aloud' as they are dealing with the diagram so that verbal as well as visual reactions are observed.

Irrespective of the particular approach chosen, learners' opinions can help provide answers to questions such as:

- how 'approachable' did the learner find the diagram?
- did the learner find it difficult to deal with for any reason?
- how interesting and aesthetically pleasing was the diagram and did it have a professional 'feel' about it?
- was the amount of information given in the diagram about right (neither overwhelming nor trivial)?
- does the learner consider this diagram (or any diagram) is necessary?
- how effective was the diagram in addressing its stated objective (assuming you have provided the learner with a statement of the diagram's purpose)?
- how well did the diagram fulfil the learner's needs at the place where it occurred in the instruction?
- how well was the diagram linked to other parts of the instructional resource?

Responses to some of these questions may require follow-up with the learner whereas others give an immediate basis for revision of the diagram. For example, if a learner says that a diagram is unapproachable, further questioning should follow to determine those features that make it difficult for the learner to engage with the diagram. However, if all respondents reject a particular diagram because it deals with a very trivial aspect of the subject matter, the course of action is obvious.

Learners' results

Before looking at how to find out about a learner's processing of a diagram, we will discuss the direct instructional results of these processes. We will take these results to be the learning that is the immediate outcome of interaction with the diagram. For example, what does the learner know after dealing with the pepper mill structure diagram that s/he did not know before?

In most instructional situations, learning is determined by formal tests on the subject matter administered before and after instruction. With a diagram, we need to be careful about the nature of these tests. For example, would we determine how well the pepper mill structure had been learned by using the learner's score on a task that involves adding the correct labels to an unlabelled structure diagram? Would matching a list of labels to the correct parts of the diagram be a satisfactory alternative? If you think about what a structure diagram is supposed to do, you may be a little uneasy about both these approaches (although each would certainly give you *some* useful information). You may also be wondering about the type of learning task that was given to the learner. Did we, for example, simply give the learner the diagram by itself and ask that it be learned for a later test? Or did we embed the diagram in the context of the instructional material of which it forms a part?

As well as giving the identity of the components that make up a structure, a structure diagram can also show aspects of the *physical form* and the *arrangement* of those entities. The labelling test described above was limited because it did not specifically explore the learner's knowledge of the appearance of the pepper mill's component parts or how they were arranged. So, by itself, it would not be a very useful basis upon which to make decisions about how such a diagram might be improved. This example illustrates the importance of thinking carefully about what you intend the diagram to do for the learner and designing the evaluation instruments so that they collect the type of information you require. What about the alternative of asking that labels and entities in the diagram only need be *matched* rather than requiring that the labels are actually *generated* by the learner? Why not do it the opposite way and have the learner generate the diagram to match given labels? What would the practical problems be in such an approach? In devising suitable strategies to evaluate the results of a diagram, we need to consider such questions and be able to provide defensible answers.

The types of questions we asked ourselves when considering evaluation of the direct outcomes of learning in this structure diagram example should also be asked for other diagram types. These questions are important not only with regard to the sorts of instruments and conditions you will use to collect evaluation information. They are also important in shaping the way you *interpret* that information. For example, if you are evaluating a concept diagram, certain superficial details of the physical appearance of the entities may not be at all important whereas the *relations* between those entities could be critical. So, in interpreting the evaluation information, appropriate weighting needs to be given to various characteristics of the learners' results.

Learners' processing

When evaluating instructional diagrams, we can investigate:

- what people do with an instructional diagram (their external behaviour)
- why they behave as they do (their internal processing).

In many cases, we will be able to use information such as opinions and test results to work out how to improve a diagram. However, sometimes we can still be mystified about why a diagram doesn't seem to be having the desired instructional effect, despite all our efforts. This is when we need to focus upon how learners might be *processing* the diagram.

Collecting information about the *results* of diagram processing is easier than collecting it about the processing itself. One of the problems is the visual nature of diagrams. Because diagrams are used as an *alternative* to words, it can be difficult for a person to say much about some of the things that are happening when s/he processes a diagram. Nevertheless, useful information can still be gathered by asking an individual learner to think aloud while working through a diagram. It is valuable to use a strategically placed video camera to record the think-aloud session and then analyse this recording to pick up clues as to what was going on in the learner's mind. If you ask the learner to point to parts of the diagram s/he is thinking about, it makes it easier to interpret what processes may have been occurring. Once you have viewed the videotape yourself a few times, it can be helpful to have the learner watch it with you and comment on what s/he was thinking about at various times.

Collection of verbal information about diagram processing can be assisted by the use of suitable probes such as 'give me a summary in your own words of what this diagram is about', or, 'show me the main sections of this diagram', or, 'tell me what this part of the diagram shows'. You can also give a person a particular learning task based on the diagram and try to determine what types of processing might be going on as s/he carries out the task.

The collection of non-verbal information about diagram processing is more difficult but potentially extremely valuable. If diagram interpretation involves processing of which a person is unaware or which is difficult to verbalize, it would be useful to have some way to tap into this processing. One approach is to ask the learner to copy and then recall a diagram. Examining the nature of the changes that occur upon copying or recall can give you clues as to why there may be problems with the diagram's instructional effectiveness. These changes may suggest things about the way the diagrams were processed. Looking at the output from such tasks allows you to answer questions such as:

- which entities were lost or changed in the processing and which were preserved?
- what sort of changes did entities undergo during processing (shape, size, orientation, position, rendering, etc)?
- at what levels are breakdowns in structure of the diagram evident (overall structure, local details, mid-level structure, etc)?

Information like this can help you to infer characteristics of the processing and provide clues as to improvements that could be made to improve a diagram or the way the diagram is supported. For example, it may indicate that the problem lies not so much with the diagram itself but with the learner's lack of background knowledge about the subject area. In such a case, an appropriate improvement may be to leave the diagram as it is but provide additional information that fills a gap in relevant background.

Learners' performance

Where diagrams are used to present a straightforward physical procedure, it may be sufficient to evaluate the effectiveness of a diagram by having the person carry out that procedure using the diagram as a guide and record where s/he has difficulty. The evaluator can note on a copy of the diagram the parts of the procedure that cause difficulty and then retrace the steps with the learner to determine what specific aspects of the diagram need to be improved.

During this retracing, detailed probes can be used to help expose why a difficulty arises. Specific activities can be given to the learner that let you see how well s/he is making connections between the diagram and what the diagram represents. For example, a request such as, 'Turn the pepper mill so that it gives me the view shown in this diagram', can let you check on how easy the learner finds it to relate the orientation in the diagram to the physical reality of the subject matter as a whole. Similar probes can be used to determine how effectively the diagram allows the learner to recognize, locate and manipulate the various entities that make up the subject matter. For example, with the aid of the diagram, the learner could be:

- given a dismantled pepper mill and asked to 'show which is the toothed wheel and which is the ribbed grinding wall' (*recognition*)
- given an assembled pepper mill and asked to 'show where to find the toothed wheel' (*location*)
- given a partly dismantled pepper mill and asked to 'remove the toothed wheel' (*manipulation*).

In other cases, such as where the subject matter of the diagram is abstract or where the learner cannot interact with it directly, other approaches must be found. Various models, simulations and other forms of representation (such as interactive video) that allow the learner to respond on the basis of the diagram are useful in these cases. The intention should be for the learner to make explicit the connections between the diagram and the other form of representation.

Gathering information

Entities

How well do learners deal with the entities in a diagram? Three important aspects to be evaluated with respect to entities are the success learners have in:

- isolating individual entities (knowing where each entity starts and ends; knowing what constitutes an entity)
- identifying each of the entities (not only being able to attach a name to the entity, but also knowing what that entity stands for in the diagram)
- characterizing the properties of the entities and interpreting their significance within the diagram.

Evaluation of success in isolating individual entities can begin by having a learner mark the boundaries of each of the labelled pieces in a diagram with a different colour. (If the diagram is not labelled, a list of parts can be provided.) This helps to pick up any confusion there may be about how far each entity extends. However, in some diagrams, a group of graphic entities together make up a larger part of the subject matter. For example, the grinding compartment of a pepper mill is made up of a toothed wheel and the ridged wall that surrounds it. It is often important that the learner can identify this type of larger composite entity, as well as the individual items it comprises. In this case, you might have the learner make several passes at the diagram. In the first, the learner marks in the basic level entities as described above and in the second, draws a ring around any of these marked entities that go together to make up a group.

When evaluating success in identifying entities, keep in mind that it may not always be particularly important that learners are able to *name* all the entities in a diagram. Sometimes it is sufficient that they know what aspect of the subject matter the entity stands for. For example, in following a diagrammatic explanation of how to dismantle a pepper mill, most of the process can be successfully performed without knowing what each of the parts is called. So, in evaluating the identification of entities, approaches may vary from requiring learners to label or verbally name indicated entities to simply pointing to the entity as the one which performs a particular function or is the next one involved in a sequence of operations.

Success in characterizing the properties of entities and their significance can be evaluated by asking questions about those entities that require the learner to go beyond what is explicitly depicted in the diagram. For example, the toothed wheel and grinding compartment in a *salt* mill are made from nylon rather than the steel that is used in a pepper mill (salt causes steel to rust away rapidly, an effect not produced by pepper). If a diagram's purpose was to help learners compare and contrast these two types of mills, it would be important that the learners could readily characterize this difference and say why it is significant. If different types of shading were used to indicate the use of nylon in the salt mill and steel in the pepper mill, the learner could be asked specific questions about what the different shading showed and why it was important.

Relations

A diagram needs to function as more than a 'visual list' of entities in order fulfil its instructional potential. Although the entities in a diagram must be readily discernible and identifiable, it is usually the way that diagrams represent the relations between these entities that gives them their explanatory power. So, a comprehensive evaluation of a diagram will determine how effectively learners can deal with these relations.

Techniques that may help gather information about relations include:

- Asking learners to point to the more important parts of the diagram, the less important parts and the parts that are different from the rest of the diagram in some way. This can

be followed up by asking why these parts are or are not important.
- Having learners explain what is wrong with a version of the diagram that has been deliberately altered with respect to some of its key relations.
- Giving learners an incomplete version of the diagram to have them discuss what is missing and what the missing parts belong to. (Remove details that form parts of important wholes.)
- Asking learners to extend a diagram beyond its current scope (in time or space).
- Having learners classify parts of the diagram into categories that they invent themselves – 'things that seem to you to belong together in some way' – and then asking them to justify their groupings.

Field testing diagrams

Ideally, a diagram designer would like to know how the learners for whom the diagram is intended will treat it in their instructional context. However, for practical reasons, it is not always possible to collect such information in the early stages of evaluation. The suggestions given above are intended only to give preliminary guidance as to how information that may be useful in an evaluation may be collected. It is emphasized that these suggestions do not claim to be comprehensive, nor do they address the complex issues associated with trying to evaluate what happens when diagrams are used in the context that actually occurs during instruction. Many of the suggested techniques are likely to be subject to strong contextual effects. So, great caution should be used in extrapolating from the decontextualized type of testing used as a tool for diagram development to realities of where and how the instructional resource which contains the diagram will be used.

Information collected about the way a diagram is processed and the outcomes of that processing typically says as much about the instructional context and material which accompany a diagram as it does about the diagram itself. Where possible, the final phase of evaluation should be carried out so as to give these influences free rein. However, even without the luxury of a field trial, much can be done to realize the undoubted potential of diagrams and help to ensure they are instructionally successful.

9 Helping the Diagram User

Making diagrams more manageable

This book concerns successful instructional diagrams and, as explained earlier, the instructional success of a diagram is only partly due to its design. Even quite poorly designed diagrams, or those that seem too difficult for a particular group of learners, can be made instructionally more effective by embedding them in a suitable context. So, as well as providing guidance for the development of new diagrams, we will look at ways to make *existing* diagrams more successful as aids to instruction. Of course the ideas we will look at here are equally applicable to new (well-designed) diagrams that you produce yourself. These ideas should be considered whenever an instructional resource is being developed that will include diagrams (especially when the target learners are unlikely to have extensive experience or high levels of skill in dealing with diagrams).

This chapter deals with approaches that can be used to help learners 'get more' from a given diagram. These approaches are intended to help learners process diagrams more effectively in a number of ways, such as the following.

- Changing learners' attitudes to diagrams so that they choose to treat them differently from the way they treat everyday pictures.
- Providing learners with general and specific strategies that can be used to handle the challenge of constructing an appropriate meaning from a diagram.
- Supporting particular diagrams with adjunct resources that will lead learners through a series of useful processing activities.

If you look back to some of the reasons given in earlier chapters as to why diagrams are ineffective, you will see that these three approaches are quite comprehensive.

Increasing learner involvement

A worst case scenario for the diagrams in an instructional resource is that the learner completely ignores them and concentrates on other modes of information presentation, such as text. We have already seen in Chapter 7 that deliberate use of 'inescapable' connections which produce a strong integration between diagrams and their companion modes of presentation can make it less likely that the learner will ignore diagrams. So, one way to help ensure that learners will engage with the diagrams you provide in an instructional resource is to weave them intimately into the fabric of that resource, rather than treating them as an afterthought.

However, it may not be enough just to provide good integration of the diagrams with the rest of an instructional package. You may need to be more prescriptive in the way you expect learners to treat the diagrams. In the following discussion, we will assume that our learners are not adept at processing the types of diagrams to be presented in the instructional package (and perhaps not even accustomed to dealing effectively with diagrams in general). If, like most instructors, you are used to thinking of diagrams as a solution to instructional problems (rather than having the potential to be problems in themselves), this perspective may be a little unfamiliar. However, when learners are faced with new subject matter, the last thing we wish to do is make life harder for them by adding diagram interpretation to their list of difficulties. So, it makes sense, especially with those who are new to a subject area, to err on the side of giving too much support rather than too little.

Having learners engage with the diagrams in a resource is a matter of quality as well as quantity. Learners usually need to do more than religiously look at every diagram that occurs in an instructional resource. What is also important is how the learners *interact* with the diagram while they are looking at it.

Your goal should be to help learners go through the sorts of mental processing of the diagram that will allow them to build up a solid understanding of the subject matter. One way to do this is to provide activities that will intensify the experience learners have of the diagram. These activities should be designed to address aspects of the diagram which are central to its representation of the subject matter. For example, some activities might help the learners to 'get a foot in the door' with the diagram by showing them a good way to begin dealing with the depiction in a productive fashion. Others might heighten their awareness of the important transformations that are incorporated in the diagram, since these are fundamental to its explanatory power. Still others might extend the learners' processing of the diagram so that this was carried out at different levels ranging from a global overview to a detailed consideration of very local aspects of the diagram.

The essence of the types of activities we should be encouraging is that they involve various types of mental *manipulation* of a diagram's constituents. Often, this will also require outward and visible processes as well. For example, we may ask the learner to add markings to a diagram, annotate particular regions of the diagram, modify the diagram so that some of its components are changed (sometimes quite extensively) or even draw completely new diagrams.

However, these activities need to be much more than 'busy work'. Their fundamental purpose must be to guide the learner through the types of mental processes that will help them to fulfil the diagram's potential as an instructional tool. Although it is true that lots of practice in activities such as redrawing a diagram or labelling it from memory can increase recall, practice alone (especially at this superficial level) is likely to have little effect on coming to grips with the content of the diagram.

When learners are faced with a particular diagram-processing task, our immediate aim is to assist them in their interpretation of a specific diagram. However, one of our longer-term goals should be to help learners become independently capable of dealing with diagrams in general in a systematic and instructionally productive manner. In some cases, it may be useful to give learners explicit guidance in the form of a checklist of questions they can ask themselves as they work with a diagram. The following are examples of such questions.

- Have I had a good look at *everything* in the diagram? (Am I being systematic, analytical and thorough?)
- What do I *already know* that may help me work out what's going on here? (Have I come across something like this before?)
- Which are the *main pieces* that make up this diagram? (How do I break it up into chunks?)
- How does each of the main chunks of the diagram give me *clues* about the other chunks? (Can I find the relations that must exist within the diagram?)
- What *special diagram techniques* have been used to depict the subject matter? (What would it be like if I could see the real thing?)

You can see that some of the above questions require the learner to know quite a lot already about how diagrams work. So, part of the process of making instructional diagrams successful is to teach learners more about diagrams in general as instructional resources. The challenge goes beyond designing better diagrams and providing more learner support for each diagram. It also involves an ongoing commitment to developing learners' visual literacy with respect to diagrams. For this reason, each diagram and its associated support materials can be seen as an opportunity to build diagram-processing knowledge and skills, not simply a means of depicting part of the subject matter in an accessible manner.

Deeper diagram processing

With many types of everyday pictures, little more than a brief, informal glance is required to process their content in an appropriate way. The reasons for this include:

- the relative familiarity of the subject matter and its unremarkable nature

- the lack of importance of most of the material in the picture (much of it being simply a background to the material of interest)
- the essentially literal representation of the subject matter.

However, diagrams are an extremely concentrated and 'artificial' form of representation which use highly abstract and conventionalized ways of depicting the subject matter. A quick glance is not usually enough for a learner to process the diagram appropriately. Everything in a well-designed diagram should have been put there for a specific reason and so everything needs to be treated as potentially important. Each entity and spatial relation has its own special significance within the diagram, and learners need to appreciate these significances. For example, the learner must be able to distinguish between entities whose role is to provide context and those that are more central to the exposition.

Close attention and careful thinking is typically required to deal with the artificiality and abstraction of a diagram; a casual approach is usually not good enough. In general, it follows that diagrams need to be *deeply processed* in order that they perform their intended instructional function properly and completely. Deep processing involves going beyond the superficial graphic characteristics of the diagram and comprehensively interpreting what those characteristics are intended to mean in terms of the subject matter that the diagram depicts.

It can be useful to draw learners' attention explicitly to the differences between a realistic representation of the subject matter (or the subject matter itself) and the various diagrammatic representations that are used. Questions that focus upon the real-life nature of the entities and relations that are shown visuo-spatially in the diagram can emphasize the highly transformed character of the depiction.

Manipulations for deeper processing

Appropriate mental manipulations of the material comprising a diagram can lead to deeper processing. The types of manipulations that may be used as the basis for learner activities in this regard could involve the learner in any of the following.

Justifying the graphic treatment of, or rendering used on, an entity within the diagram We have seen that diagrams use various visual cues to signal to the viewer how the material it contains should be interpreted. For example, in the structure diagram of the pepper mill presented in Chapter 1 (Figure 1.4), different types of shading were used to distinguish different regions (empty space, wood, metal). These were not intended to be taken literally as indicating the actual appearance of these regions. A literal interpretation of such graphic aspects of a diagram is less likely if learners are required to give an explanation of the purpose of each in terms of the way they are used to help the diagram explain its subject matter.

Classifying the entities used in the diagram We have seen that diagrams typically use entities that can be grouped into several broad categories. These include: visible and invisible parts of the subject matter; interpretation aids and graphic instructions such as dotted lines, boxes and arrows; and coding devices such as shading. Activities that give learners the task of classifying diagram components into these categories not only help to ensure that they examine all entities in the diagram: they also prepare the learners to treat these functionally distinct entities differently in the interpretation of the diagram. Learners can identify entities belonging to different groups by marking them with distinctive tags (using different colours, numbers, symbols etc).

Comparing different representations of the same subject matter These comparisons could be between realistic and diagrammatic representations, between diagrams showing different views, between diagrams that have different purposes, and so on. For example, Figure 9.1 requires learners to match the entities shown in two different views of the pepper mill's grinding mechanism. Their task is to draw lines that connect corresponding entities in the two diagrams. To do this successfully, they have to examine each of the depictions carefully: this rules out the sort of superficial approach that might be used for less abstract representations. As well as encouraging a thorough and thoughtful approach to the diagram (helping learners to

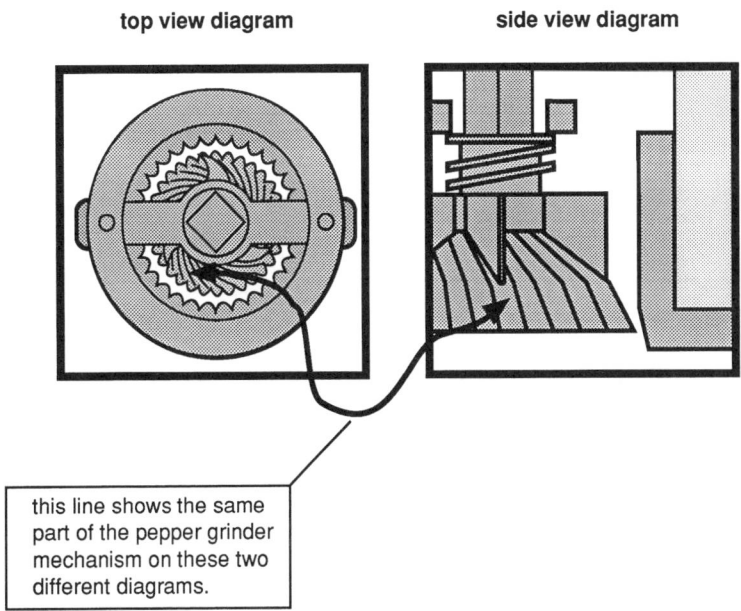

Figure 9.1 *Learners draw in connecting lines as per example to show which pieces correspond in the two different views. This encourages more intensive exploration and integration of material.*

'really get to know' the diagram), this task encourages integration of different representations of the same subject matter.

A variant of this approach is shown in Figure 9.2 (overleaf) where individual depictions are closely related in some way but do not show exactly the same subject matter. Here the aim is for learners to develop a higher-level conceptual understanding by thinking about the topic in a more abstract fashion.

*Comparing different parts of the **same** diagram* This approach can be used to encourage learners to consider *all* the entities in the diagram (rather than taking some for granted or glossing over them). It can also help them to make the relations within the

Figure 9.2 *Rather than drawing parts of a diagram themselves, learners can mark key aspects. This requires them to generalize their knowledge across depictions of superficially different examples.*

diagram (*internal* relations) more explicit. For example, Figure 9.3 asks the learner to put into words the difference between the two types of arrow used in the diagram originally shown as Figure 4.2 and the two depictions of the peppercorn. It also asks the learners to spell out the relations between some of the entities in the diagram. This type of approach can be used to focus the learner's attention on those entities and relations that you consider to be central to a proper understanding of the diagram.

Making modifications to existing diagrams This might involve learners in mentally *changing the structure* of a system so that it is capable of performing different functions or leaving the structure alone and *changing the state* of the system. For example, Figure 9.4 (on page 130) involves a change in state that requires learners to think about the effect that the entities have on each

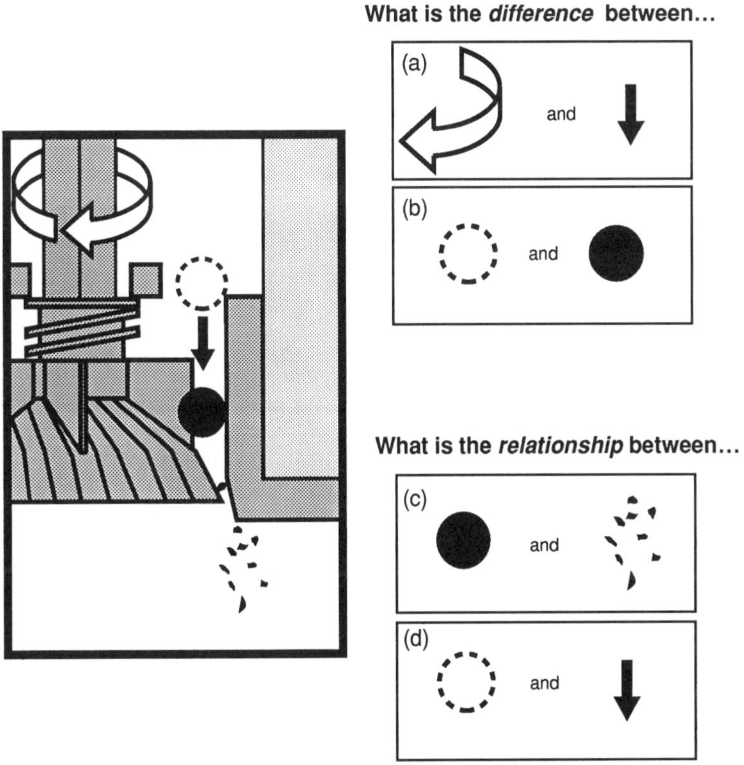

Figure 9.3 *Requiring learners to spell out explicitly the diagram's internal relations can engage them in deeper processing of the diagram's contents and draw their attention to key entities and relations.*

other when the system operates. It encourages them to consider the real-life characteristics of the entities portrayed in the diagram and the practical consequences of relations that exist between them.

Linking the material in the diagram to existing background knowledge
There are many occasions where learners already know something that will help them deal with a diagram. However, they may not appreciate that this knowledge is useful and so fail to

SUCCESSFUL INSTRUCTIONAL DIAGRAMS

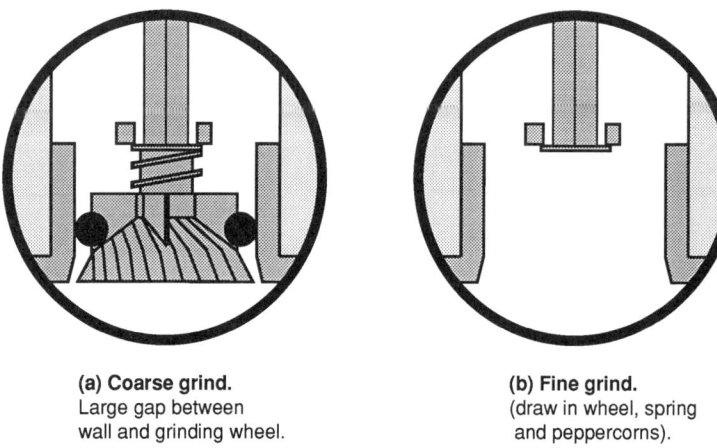

(a) **Coarse grind.**
Large gap between
wall and grinding wheel.

(b) **Fine grind.**
(draw in wheel, spring
and peppercorns).

Figure 9.4 *Learners complete diagram (b) to show change in the position of the grinding wheel and peppercorns and the compression of the spring when mill is reset to produce fine grinding.*

build *external relations* that link it with the diagram. Activities designed to activate this background knowledge can help to make a diagram less abstract and give the learner ways to make it more meaningful. If learners can say to themselves 'I see; this adjustment knob on the pepper grinder is a bit like the handle on a water tap where you turn it to alter the fineness of the water stream that comes out', or, 'Yes, I can remember buying black pepper that came ready packaged in its own disposable plastic pepper mill. As I recall, you couldn't vary the fineness of grind so I suppose all the adjustment part of the mechanism that's shown in this diagram would have been missing'. You can see from these examples how asking learners to explore analogies and make comparisons with related (but different) subject matter from their own experience can help them process a diagram more effectively. What sorts of activities could you present to learners to set them up to build these external relations?

Transforming aspects of the diagram into another representational form Asking learners to find a different way to express the diagram's graphic entities and relations requires them both to analyse the existing diagrammatic representation carefully and to develop a way to articulate its essential aspects. For example, if we gave learners a purely diagrammatic set of instructions about how to fill a pepper mill, their task could be to develop a purely text-based explanation of the process.

There are many other types of activities that you can devise which would be equally suitable for helping learners to process a diagram more effectively. The important point to keep in mind when developing such activities is that their purpose should be to stimulate the types of mental manipulation of the diagram which lead to appropriate forms of deeper processing. The activities are only as good as the amount and type of thinking they produce. So, they need to be developed carefully to demand a high level of mental engagement from the learner.

Imagery

Much of the content depicted in diagrams has an intrinsically visual character which determines that a pictorial rather than (say) a textual treatment is most appropriate. This means that *visual* comprehension and memory is part of what is required to develop a proper understanding of the subject matter and be able to recall it effectively. Some prominent researchers on learning from visual material maintain that we have both visual and non-visual aspects to our memory. They suggest that our minds store some information in the form of images and some information in a far more abstract 'propositional' form that represents facts and how they are related. Although these two memory stores are linked, each has its own particular strengths for handling information.

One approach to helping learners deal with diagrams is to encourage them to develop well-formed mental images from a diagram. These images can be of two main types:

- images of the diagram itself

- images of the real-life situation that the diagram represents.

In the former type of image the focus is on the graphic characteristics of the diagram such as the type and location of the entities, the overall appearance of each entity, any special distinguishing characteristics that are present, how the entities are arranged and grouped, etc. In the latter the idea is to go beyond the diagram and mentally construct a fleshed-out representation of the situation, putting back the sorts of things that have been left out in the process of developing the diagram. This may even extend as far as making a *dynamic mental model* from a static diagram of the situation which can be 'run' forward and backward in the mind to generate inferences and predictions.

Notice that the first of these image types is concerned with the *superficial visuo-spatial characteristics* of the diagram while the second is concerned with the *meaning* of those characteristics in terms of the subject matter represented. If the learner is faced with recalling and using a particular diagram in a problem-solving or transfer situation, both types of information are important. The diagram must not only be remembered accurately in terms of its graphical constituents and their arrangement. Their significance must also be understood so that the learner can *apply* that knowledge successfully. This involves an appreciation of the limitations and strengths of the diagram as a tool for thinking about the situation in which it will be used.

In some cases, a series of interrelated diagrams is used to present a series of different views or aspects of a given piece of subject matter. In this case the learner can be encouraged to develop mental images that integrate these different diagrams into a coherent whole. A very simple application of this approach would be to blend a series of successive diagrams about the changes an object undergoes into a continuous mental animation. For example, the two parts of the diagram in Chapter 5 showing how a pepper mill's fineness of grind is adjustable could be elaborated mentally into a continuous process.

10 Conclusion

In dealing with the requirements for successful instructional diagrams, this book has emphasized both the *quality of diagram design* and the need to give learners *high-quality support* in using diagrams effectively. We have seen that, for many learners, even well-designed diagrams should not be assumed to have some 'magical' instructional effectiveness just because they are a pictorial form of presentation. Diagrams are extremely specialized in the way they present information and so cannot be treated the same way as more everyday pictures. Neither can they be expected to act as 'stand-alone' resources which are essentially self-explanatory, especially where learners who are new to diagrams are involved. Instructional diagrams need to be seen as part of a wider instructional system. To be an effective part of that system, they must be carefully integrated with other aspects of instruction so that the learner can gain maximum benefit from the instructional resource as a whole.

As with any other component of instruction, good design is fundamental to the success of a diagram. The design and development process should bring together people who contribute different types of expertise, ranging from the subject expert, who specifies the content matter, to the artist and the media consultant who create the diagram in its finished form. Central to the successful coordination of these contributors is an instructional designer who has a thorough understanding of the opportunities and constraints that characterize the use of diagrams in instructional resources. It is the task of the instructional designer to help develop productive compromises between the sometimes very different perspectives of those involved in the process of developing a diagram. The instructional designer's final responsibility is to the learners who will be trying to use a diagram to help them understand or remember the subject matter. As with any other tool, to be effective a diagram must be well suited to its purpose, soundly constructed and appropriate for its intended users. Instructional diagrams should not only incorporate general principles of effective diagram design, they also need to have been properly evaluated in terms of the target learners.

As well as ensuring that the learner is supplied with the right diagram tool for the job, the instructional designer should also provide support in the proper use of that tool. The basis for an informed approach to providing appropriate support is an understanding of the way learners process diagrams in their instructional context. This support may be as much about helping learners approach diagram interpretation tasks in a productive manner as it is about the content represented by a particular diagram. Support provided for learners can be seen as part of the process of helping learners develop the specialized knowledge and skills that are required to handle diagrams in general in an effective manner. An important goal in providing support is to give the learners opportunities for high quality, mentally demanding interactions with diagrams that help them with deep level processing of the subject matter represented.

This book has been able to introduce you to only some of the complexities associated with the use of diagrams in instruction. It has shown you that for diagrams to be instructionally successful, the instructional designer needs to strike the difficult balance between simplifying the way the subject matter is presented and providing sufficient support. Central to achieving an effective balance is to keep the learners and their instructional context in mind at all times.

Bibliography

Brody, P J (1984). 'In search of instructional utility: A function-based approach to pictorial research'. *Instructional Science, 13*, 47–61.

Duchastel, P and Waller, R (1979). 'Pictorial illustration in instructional texts'. *Educational Technology, 19*(11), 20–25.

Fleming, M L (1987). 'Displays and communication'. In R M Gagne (Ed.), *Instructional technology: Foundations*. Hillsdale, NJ: Erlbaum.

Goldsmith, E (1984). *Research into illustration: an approach and a review*. Cambridge: Cambridge University Press.

Gombrich, E H (1990). 'Pictorial instructions'. In J Miller (Ed.), *Images and understanding* (pp 26–45). Cambridge: Cambridge University Press.

Lowe, R K (1989). 'Search strategies and inference in the exploration of scientific diagrams'. *Educational Psychology, 9*(1), 27–44.

Lowe, R K (1991). 'Expository illustrations: A new challenge for reading instruction'. *Australian Journal of Reading, 14*, 215–26.

Mandl, H and Levin, J R (Eds) (1989). *Knowledge acquisition from text and pictures*. North Holland: Elsevier.

Mayer, R E and Gallini, J K (1990). 'When is an illustration worth ten thousand words?'. *Journal of Educational Psychology, 82*, 715–26.

Pettersson, R (1989). *Visuals for information*. Englewood Cliffs, NJ: Educational Technology Publications.

Salomon, G (1979) *Interaction of media, cognition and learning*. San Francisco: Jossey-Bass.

Sless, D (1981). *Learning and visual communication*. London: Croom Helm.

Winn, W.D. (1987). 'Charts, graphs and diagrams in educational materials'. In D M Willows and H A Houghton (Eds), *The psychology of illustration: Vol. 1*, (pp 152–98). New York: Springer-Verlag.

Winn, W D and Sutherland, S W (1989). 'Factors influencing the recall of elements in maps and diagrams, and the strategies used to encode them'. *Journal of Educational Psychology, 81*, 33–9.

Index

Added information 27, 43
Advantages of diagrams 17
Animation 90, 92
Arrows 69
Artwork 38, 48, 65, 107

Background knowledge 30

Colour 84
Computer-based diagrams 88
Conceptual diagram 58
Content analysis 52
Context 20, 44, 45

Design 47
Diagram characteristics 12
Diagram conventions 32
Diagram dangers 40
Diagram development 38
Diagram devices 36
Diagram failure 21, 34
Diagram improvement 106
Diagram justifications 40, 47
Diagram knowledge 24, 29
Diagram processing 25
Diagram production 64
Diagram production aids 79
Diagram reading skills 24
Diagram specifications 39
Diagram vocabulary 31
Diagrams and text 99
Diagrams versus other pictures 29
Diagrams versus text 27
Disadvantages of diagrams 18

Empty space 73
Entities 29, 52, 53, 66, 69, 70, 117
Essential information 42
Evaluation 106, 108, 117
Explanation 60
External information 25, 28
External relations 37

Field testing 119

Graphic components 16
Graphic design 21, 47, 107
Graphic treatment 70
Guiding diagram processing 100

Imagery 131
Information gaps 43
Information limits 42
Information presentation 26, 50
Instructional design 47, 107
Instructional effectiveness 34
Instructional functions 49
Instructional objectives 55
Instructional purpose 20
Integrating diagrams 95, 97, 102, 104

Interaction quality 89, 122
Interactivity 88
Internal information 25, 28, 30
Internal relations 36
Interpretation 44

Labels 69
Layout 74
Learner activity 51, 89, 122, 125
Learner control 86
Learner's opinions 111
Learner's performance 116
Learner's processing 114
Learner's results 112
Levels of meaning 35, 71
Literal interpretation 35

Meaning 43
Meaningful learning 12
Media 82
Media constraints 83, 87
Media consultant 108

Non-redundant encoding 17
Non-spatial relations 75
Non-visual relations 55

Objectives 56
Omitted information 27, 43

Process diagram 14, 15, 47

Processing depth 124

Qualifiers 52, 55

Realistic depiction 12, 26, 29
Redundant encoding 16
Relations 31, 75, 118
Relationships 52, 53, 55, 70
Remembering 12
Resolution 83

Spatial arrangement 74
Static diagrams 91
Structure diagram 14, 15
Subject expert 107
Support for the learner 96, 121
Symbols 31

Target learners 20, 22
Text and diagrams 97
Text components 16
Transformations 14, 35, 59

Understanding 12

Video 87
Visual literacy 24
Visual relations 55
Visuo-spatial characteristics 54